A Broken and Contrite Heart

EFFIE DARLENE BARBA

authorHOUSE®

AuthorHouse™
1663 Liberty Drive
Bloomington, IN 47403
www.authorhouse.com
Phone: 1-800-839-8640

First published by AuthorHouse 4/21/2011

ISBN: 978-1-4567-5589-8 (e)
ISBN: 978-1-4567-5590-4 (sc)

Printed in the United States of America

A Broken and Contrite Heart
Copyright
Registration TXu001700645
Effective Date of Registration 8/31/2010

Front Cover Portrait "A Broken and Contrite Heart"
by Ronald Bertrand Barba used by permission
Copyright VAu001055541
Effective Date of Registration 01/25/2011

Unless otherwise indicated, Bible quotations are taken from
King James (version{s}) of the Bible.
As indicated, The Holy Bible, New International Version, NIV Copyright @1973, 1978,
1984, 2011 by Biblica, Inc. Used by permission. All rights reserved worldwide.

Dedication

*T*oday, August 28, 2010; as I typed the closing poem of Chapter 10; I realized this book is done. It was many years ago that God whispered in my heart that I was to write this book and at the time I began; yet, I recurrently stumbled at some of the thoughts or words. Now, as I look back over all the incidences of my life since then; I must say God had a plan. The idea of the book was always lingering in an area of my brain; though never completed until now. I realize as I review the last 5 years of my life, God was preparing me for the climax of this book. He has walked me through each step of the way from the jail ministry to a careful review of my own short comings. He has provided me with worship songs such as those written and performed by Keith and Krysten Getty, sometimes with the help of Stuart Townsend. The words to each of their songs rang with such truth and hope. Then there was the day that I by sheer chance had heard that there was a pastor named John Piper who did a 9 month series on Romans and I knew I had to hear him. He became a tremendous mentor for me. I listened carefully through Romans, Seeing and Savoring Christ and his book "Future Grace". Each step, each detail of my life was to bring me ever closer to the magnificent truths I needed to know to further explain suffering and failures through the eyes of Christ. I had to be unchained from all prosperity gospels' lies and the lies of legalism that had kept me defeated from the victory that was meant to be mine. I thank God for this opportunity to have been given this life filled and overflowing with opportunities to know Him better. I dedicate this book to Melissa Smith, my beautiful daughter who truly shows God through service and never ceases to amaze me with her beautiful spirit. To Alberto Barba, who is the truest of leaders demonstrating fully his spiritual gifts of leadership and exhortation with such wisdom that only God could have revealed so much to him—he exudes the joy and exuberance of Christian living. And to Ronald Barba who as the unique blend of justice and mercy who displays a faith so strong and uncompromising that I am awed at the very sight of it. And of course, I must also thank my mother who first told me about Christ so many years ago. She continues to live with me and praises God despite her battling with manic depressive disorder and advanced arthritis. I must also say a thank you to both Rochelle Robinson and Nancy McGuire who have been my encouragers as they were sent each draft for proofreading.

Table of Contents

Introduction

This is a book that lays heavy on my heart and I only pray that God guide each word so as to help all who have ever felt the weight of a broken heart. Suffering and sorrow is a subject which I have known too well in my lifetime; yet, can I consider that an honor that God would love me so much as to have wanted to truly show me the depth and the breath of His heart? Can you fully understand the heart of God until you come to the fullest realization of the depth of pain He feels? I had faced many battles in my lifetime including abuse, cancer, chronic illness, financial disaster, separation from my daughter, and widowhood. Through all of it, God had guided and provided me with His joy, His wisdom, and His strength. Having lived victoriously through so many difficulties and having seen His provision, I guess I must have become complacent in His grace. Then one faithful or perhaps faithless day I awakened from my spiritual sleep and suddenly became overwhelmed by how many times I had broken God's heart. Through all the years of trials and suffering, I had at moments cried out "why?" He always came and provided the answer and I continued to praise Him. Then I began to believe that God owed me the desires of my heart for all my faithfulness. Such a foolish thought, but pride usually is the beginning of sin in a believer's heart. Was that not the case in both David's and Simon Peter's life? Oddly, it slipped in so quietly, as I had not considered myself to be proud. Still if I was to be used by God fully, I needed to be readjusted, broken and then restored with His truth. I needed to grasp the depth of His love for me and confront sin with a new awareness of its devastating effects on our Christian walk. I, like David and Peter, needed to learn what it meant to have a broken spirit. I needed to learn what it was to have a broken and contrite heart. Still I was not quite prepared for what was about to happen.

A few years ago, I was betrayed by someone that I loved and trusted. Still that was not the worst of it. You see, I was forced to come face to face with my own sin; the initial guilt of which I felt unbearable. I had desired the relationship to become more than it was, allowing loneliness to drive me. When God had stepped in and allowed him to betray me, I became angry with God for breaking my heart once more. I forgot that God's plan was best and I had made lame excuses for myself. Well, actually, I lied to myself. When I realized my friend had betrayed me, I reacted with anger and jealousy toward this my friend; I sent one e-mail that struck a crushing blow. Oh, true he had betrayed me and lied to me. Still my unchristian response broke what I had believed to be a long time testimony of God's mercy, grace, and unconditional love. It is funny how when we excuse one sin in our life we become so confused in our thinking. How could I have failed God so desperately? I, who had proclaimed His name to everyone I met. Each morning I had spent two hours in devotional study and prayer. I had walked a thousand valleys, fallen many times; yet, understood His grace, His love. When I couldn't see where the money would come from to pay the bills, I with great faith gave Him His portion and beyond. I always knew He would provide. Amazingly, God still used me to testify of Him, but I had been living a lie. The sad part was, at that moment I couldn't even recognize it. Satan has a way of making us think that all is ok, and that our little sin is insignificant within the scheme of things. He even makes us think that perhaps it is not even sin. I thought that I understood my frailty and even prayed the warrior's prayer each morning. Still I failed the one true love for I had failed God. I knew all about grace, but I needed to learn a new appreciation for sin. As I had fallen to my knees completely broken, I had wondered if there was any way to ever stand up again. I fell before His throne of grace and poured out in prayer the depth of my pain and sorrow. Could I ever be used of God again? My failure lay heavy on my heart and I thought there was no way to stand up again.

All my hopes and dreams lay shattered at my feet. You see after so many years of growth, sorrows, and victories in Him as a Christian I had seen my friend as a gift from God at the ending of a tumultuous and stormy life, a gift for my humble faithfulness as His servant. It is foolish to believe that God owed me anything. So even more this loss and betrayal felt like God had turned His back on me; yet I knew better. I knew that God's grace and mercy were dependent on Him, who He is not on who I am. I lay there broken and shattered at His throne of grace. There it was that God gently reached out His hand of love to stroke my hair and whisper His words of love, again. He slowly and steadily restored me as He taught me a deeper knowledge of His heart and mind. I suddenly had realized that throughout these years that I had asked "God, why do you allow my heart to be so broken?" I had failed to understand the truth. The truth, in all its depth and depravity was, "Why have I so broken your heart, Lord?" You see, "Jesus wept" because He knew that He had brought to Mary, Martha, and His friends the greatest gift of all; but they didn't see it. Each time that I was so caught up in what I wanted and asked why; I imagine that again Jesus wept. I failed to understand and see Him for who He is and that my failure broke His heart. He has been standing there all the time and saying, "Child, I am here, I have the best for you, only trust me." He stood there with all I needed and I kept saying I needed more.

It was at that time that I had begun to write this book; perhaps had I finished it then, I would have not fallen to the same sin. Or perhaps, I was still not broken enough or ready to face the truth straight forward. I separated myself to God, believing that I was avoiding sin for a long time. The next time I fell into the same pit was at a time I believed myself to have grown enough to not be fooled so quickly by Satan. Yet, there he was lurking in the background, just waiting for his moment. It came next at a time in which I was very busy about God's work and for once was not looking for anything else. I was filled with joy and hope. My life began to prosper. Did I become complacent? I am not sure. This time someone entered my life that was very dear. Although he gave the appearance of always being happy, he was plagued by great financial problems due to multiple bad choices and a tumultuous life created by bad choices. Once more, God's warrior headed forth to rescue and save someone. I with prayer was certain that God wanted this; still, I fumbled with the delivery. I took the job at hand, not awaiting the instructions as to how, and ran straightforward ahead. I didn't wait for God to clear the path or build the bridge. So when I lunged off the cliff into the whirling waters, I was stunned. More than that, I spent months trying to justify my actions rather than to face them directly with God. I began to feel like a phony Christian. I tried to continue my ministry (amazingly God still used me); but inside that whirling river I was drowning and too ashamed to cry for help this time. Slowly, but surely I began to plunge into a deep depression. I found myself to be wavering in my ability to be kind. I became angry at times at the very person I had started out wanting to help. Mean and hateful words are not the way to show God's mercy and grace. I finally awoke from my own lies and had to walk away; hurting the one I had meant to help and leaving behind a testimony that only God can repair. My question then was "So, now God, where do I go from here?" Still I know He is the great restorer and has a plan for my life. It is with great humility that I now reveal to you the answers that He has given me in the scripture and pray that my frank honesty may help someone else in need.

Somewhere in the faulty interpretation of scripture, I believed that if I could work hard enough and by doing so please God; then, He would give me the desire of my heart. That desire was someone to love me completely someone who would adore me. So I spent my life filled with either a false belief that God did not really love me; even though He had saved me—He didn't really totally love me waffling with a deep sense of loneliness. I always believed that no matter how hard I tried, I would not be good enough for Him to really love me and that was why He did not give me this one thing. I can imagine that it was a deep sense of loneliness and inadequacy that plagued the woman at the well. A friend once told me that I misunderstood God that because of my faith and devotion, it was actually that God loved me so much He couldn't bear to share me. Yet, I couldn't believe that because I felt so inadequate. I would watch some older couple with the husband teetering around the hospital bed with so much love and care for his sick wife and inside I felt great pangs of jealousy.

I did have the opportunity to marry the love of my life; yet, due to his own emotional fears he had throughout the 16 year marriage told me that he did not love me. He said that he had married me because he knew I would be a good wife and mother. Then one bright day, he proclaimed how much he had always loved me and that I was the best thing that ever happened in his life—the next day he died and I asked God, "Why?"

Have you, my friend, ever been at that point of despair? Has your heart been so broken that you feel the morning can never come? Have you felt the pain of losing something you loved and couldn't understand why? Have you ever felt the weight of knowing you broke God's heart? Have you ever failed so badly that you see no way back? If so, walk this journey with me for we are in great company with David, Paul, Moses, Abraham, Peter and I daresay a large audience of great men and women of God.

The pain that comes from a broken and contrite heart for God may in part be explained by our need to grow up. Many good meaning Christians will say that all of our sorrow or trials are God's punishment for our sin. I have learned a lot about sorrow in my lifetime and know that this is not true. I will attempt to address sorrow in one section of this book as well. The broken and contrite heart is different from our tribulations and sorrows. It is when you have blatantly failed God. Even then, there may be natural consequences to that sin, but God is standing with open arms of Love to restore you not lightning bolts to knock you down. Grace is not by works and is a free gift. Ephesians 2 "8For by grace are ye saved through faith; and that not of yourselves: it is the gift of God:

9Not of works, lest any man should boast"

I also wondered why God allowed this to happen if I was continuously seeking Him. After all, as with Peter or Job, Satan could not touch them or "sift them" without God allowing it. This is shown in the first chapters of Job and again within Luke 22:31-32 "31 And the Lord said, Simon, Simon, behold, Satan hath desired to have you, that he may sift you as wheat. 32 But I have prayed for thee, that thy faith fail not: and when thou art converted, strengthen thy brethren." So back to my question, "Why didn't God stop me?" Was there something hidden in the recesses of my spirit that needed to be addressed, something only He could change only by allowing me to be sifted by Satan? Perhaps, something I had kept hidden even from myself. My heart over time had been so broken. I still struggled with the belief that I had to work to become good enough to be loved. I still struggled with legalism. In my mind, I knew the truth of God's love; but I needed a heart transplant. My heart was so scared that it could scarcely pump through the arteries in a way to empower my Christian life. I had been in desperate need of a heart transplant that I might truly live out the joy and peace that He meant to pulsate through my entire life. All the years of sorrow and pain still being seen through legalistic eyes had stripped the joy out of my bleeding heart. In my mind, I knew the truth; but I needed a heart that could also rest in His truth.

Still for those who have not had to confront their own frailty, what about all the pain and sorrow that remains a part of every Christian's life? Does God have a plan in the midst of broken dreams, pain, and suffering? Can God still use someone who has utterly failed Him in their Christian walk?

This I do know that great faith is learned through great pain and sorrow. In this God had blessed me beyond measure. For He chose me, He trusted me to walk the road I have; in the center of which He has revealed Himself–His heart to me. I would walk each of those former sorrows and shed each tear again for the excellence of knowing Him in all His glory. Still, understanding this and victoriously having overcome many valleys of sorrow had not prevented me from falling to Satan's whispers. That is the deepest of pain that can be felt by one who loves God and the worst part is that the guilt within this sorrow whispers back to me and you "this was entirely your own fault." Can God still have had a plan that includes our restoration after our own sin caused us to plummet to the ground? Perhaps it is David and Simon Peter that expresses the truth in this matter in its greatest form. When sitting in that moment of desperation I wrote this song which expresses the depth of what I felt; perhaps, like David in Psalm 51.

DIDN'T I LOVE YOU ENOUGH

David had seen the hand of God
Guide His every step
He now was king of Israel
What wondrous grace he knew
And then he sinned
And broke God's heart
So far away he strayed
And then he must have prayed

Chorus: Didn't I love You enough, Lord?
Didn't I trust You enough?
Didn't I reach out my hand, Lord
And seek you enough?
Lord search out my heart
Sift out the chaff
Prune me and mold me
Restore me again
Open my eyes
That I might see you
Teach me to love you
As you have loved me

I studied your word
I walked in your grace
I prayed and I tithed
And I witnessed of you
In the midst of this moment
I failed you, Oh Lord
Your heart I did break
The pain too much for me

Chorus: Didn't I love You enough, Lord?
Didn't I trust You enough?
Didn't I reach out my hand, Lord
And seek you enough?
Lord search out my heart
Sift out the chaff
Prune me and mold me
Restore me again
Open my eyes
That I might see you
Teach me to love you
As you have loved me

So I bring you my sin
This heart crushed within
I lay it before you
At the foot of your cross
Now I can see You
The depth of your love
Your heart that was crushed
From your love just for me

Chorus: Didn't I love You enough, Lord?
Didn't I trust You enough?

Didn't I reach out my hand, Lord
And seek you enough?
Lord search out my heart
Sift out the chaff
Prune me and mold me
Restore me again
Open my eyes
That I might see you
Teach me to love you
As you have loved me

I stand in this darkness
I can't see Your light
So, please take my hand, Lord
Let me hear your command, Lord
Guide my step forward
Help me walk toward Your light
That I might now feel You
Your arms hold me tight

Chorus: Didn't I love You enough, Lord?
Didn't I trust You enough?
Didn't I reach out my hand, Lord
And seek you enough?
Lord search out my heart
Sift out the chaff
Prune me and mold me
Restore me again
Open my eyes
That I might see you
Teach me to love you
As you have loved me

Can He still keep the remainder of the promise in Ephesians 2. [10]For we are his workmanship, created in Christ Jesus unto good works, which God hath before ordained that we should walk in them" Can He take my sin, my failure and my brokenness and make me look like Him, when I lay them at His feet? I say yes, a thousand times yes. I daresay that He knew each time I would fail Him and I have not surprised Him any of the time and He has always been standing ready with the restoration even before I fell. In fact, He knew how to take my failure and turn it around into His Glory every time.

CHAPTER 1

Broken Spirit

Psalm 51

16For thou desirest not sacrifice; else would I give it: thou delightest not in burnt offering.

17The sacrifices of God are a **broken spirit: a broken and a contrite heart**, O God, thou wilt not despise"

*H*ow do we reconcile that this God of mercy, love and grace should ever desire a broken spirit or a broken heart for any of His children? Is this a contradiction to the very concept of grace? Did not this same God say "Therefore being justified by faith we have peace with God through our Lord Jesus Christ. By whom also we have access by faith into this grace wherein we stand and rejoice in the hope of the glory of God." Romans 5:1-2 Broken spirit, broken and contrite heart, peace, rejoice-is it possible to reconcile all these words as being the same God's intention for his children? Can a broken spirit and heart rejoice in peace? These questions have haunted most of my Christian life; yet, only recently have I come to realize that a broken spirit, broken heart and contrite heart referred to in Psalms is not about the Christian's suffering that is a part of our life on this earth. There was a time that I confused the two as being the same. Instead this verse points directly to that moment that you fall completely prostrate before God and declare your complete and utter failure in walking this Christian walk. It is when you have truly come to the very end of yourself stripped of all your pride and valor.

Why is it that I who so understand that my salvation is based on Grace alone-not of myself; then why must I struggle so in this Christian walk. So often it has felt that despite my devotion, my study of the word, and all the faith He has so freely given me; I still would take three steps forward only to stumble back four. Perhaps I had even come to accept this to be a part of life on earth and part of the growing process. Yet, this time I came face to face with my total nothingness that I might find being in Him. How can it be that God still chooses to bless me and use me in spite of my failures?

So many years ago I wrote "Mountaintop Experiences in the Valley-for those who live their lifetime in the valleys" In it I had preserved God's answer to pain, sorrow, loneliness, guilt and letting go of those whom you love. You would have thought being equipped with such knowledge would have protected me. Yet, understanding His word had not made me immune to the frailties of this human body in which I live.

Later I wrote "God's Inspiration-a simple plan of Love" In it is laid the simplicity of walking the Christian life that God requires only loving God, prayer, bible study and let Him do the rest. Again equipped with such intimate knowledge of Him; I should have soared above these fleshly struggles and I seemed to for a while. Strangely enough, when I felt the closest to Him is when the war within me began again. Initially, I began excusing myself for some small sin which I confessed and moved on, that is I thought I did. Yet, perhaps I had failed to see the magnitude of what sin does to a Christian. Perhaps I failed to realize and remember that Satan is constantly trying to destroy my testimony and my life, That was something Peter had learned with a broken and contrite heart as he wrote, "Be sober, be vigilant; because your adversary the devil, as a roaring lion walketh about seeking whom he may devour" I Peter 5:8.

Still only 2 verses later in I Peter 5:10 he writes, "But the God of all grace, who hath called us unto His eternal glory by Christ Jesus, after that ye have suffered a while, make you perfect, stablish, strengthen, settle you." He had found this secret after his great failure and restoration. He was proof that God could restore and use a Christian and in fact, change that person into someone very useful for the kingdom.

Could Peter have ever carried out his commission to preach the gospel had he not fallen broken heartedly before Christ; having failed Him; and then felt His forgiveness? Despite having walked with Christ, his own pride and selfish desires stood in the way of his understanding the true mission of Christ. He had to be brought to the end of his own self before he could be truly used of God. He had to learn how really small he was and how really big God is. He needed to understand the depth of grace and mercy which Christ showed Him with such patience and love in order to truly proclaim the Gospel. He had a truly big job before him and it was necessary that he no longer had even a shred of his own pride or will. He had to die to himself before he could live to God.

David with such passion, such faith in God that he could slay a giant; yet, walked such a path of victories and failures, joys and sorrows. He also came to the point of complete brokenness, recognizing that the greatest heartbreak that can exist is recognizing that "I broke God's heart". Still, he is known as a "man after God's own heart" The songs of David remain forever some of the most comforting words of the Bible. They remind us of how frail we really are and how gracious, mighty and loving is our Heavenly Father, deserving of praise.

So there is still hope for me and for anyone of you who struggles or has struggled in this same way. In fact, an extensive review of the scripture would reveal that in most cases there are more of us than there are those who get it right. Please do not misunderstand this and search out sin so that you might fail before being used. There are the examples of Joseph and Daniel and Esther who found their close walk with God without such examples of failures as I, but for those of us who do fail-we can have hope of restoration. Again, do not misunderstand me to say this is an excuse for failure, merely, that this is perhaps the key to understanding the mystery between brokenness and joy.

There are some very distinct steps necessary to being restored. One is to quit lying to your own self and to God. You must go before Him stripped of all your excuses and ask His forgiveness. Then draw yourself aside buried in scripture and prayer for whatever time is necessary to have your joy restored. This will vary from person to person. During this time period you must equip yourself with His armor. Then equipped with God's armor, once more you can emerge as His warrior for Christ. Rather you allow Him to emerge through you. You must learn the necessity of dying to self that He might live through you. Also, you must see the difference between this temporary world and eternity; never losing sight of where your home truly is and whom is your true love. Never forget how easily you fell and never get lulled into the idea that it cannot happen again. Let me assure you, it can.

Another major problem is our inflated image as to who we are and our limited image as to who God really is. We make him too small or we try to make Him the puppet to our own wishes and desires, rather than we being the servant to His desires. Somehow we see Him as the one who is there to grant our wishes, not remembering that He knows what a chaotic mess we will make of our lives if it all went our way. He knows us perfectly well. David reflects this in Psalms 139:1-10

1O lord, thou hast searched me, and known me.
²Thou knowest my downsitting and mine uprising, thou understandest my thought afar off.
³Thou compassest my path and my lying down, and art acquainted with all my ways.
⁴For there is not a word in my tongue, but, lo, O LORD, thou knowest it altogether.

⁵Thou hast beset me behind and before, and laid thine hand upon me.
⁶Such knowledge is too wonderful for me; it is high, I cannot attain unto it.
⁷Whither shall I go from thy spirit? or whither shall I flee from thy presence?
⁸If I ascend up into heaven, thou art there: if I make my bed in hell, behold, thou art there.
⁹If I take the wings of the morning, and dwell in the uttermost parts of the sea;
¹⁰Even there shall thy hand lead me, and thy right hand shall hold me.

Let me try to break this down. O Lord, you have searched every part of my being and you know me now—from before the foundations of this earth and to eternity you know everything about me. You have always known every time I would utterly fail and each time you would lift me up. You have known my thoughts even before I existed. You have surrounded my path of life and even surrounded me when I laid down my armor to quit. You are acquainted with all my idiosyncrasies, all that makes me uniquely me. There is not a word that I have spoken but what You knew even before I said it. You even know every word yet unuttered that will come from my tongue. You have besieged me, surrounded me. You know all my past, my present and my future. You have laid your hand upon me. How can I ever be able to comprehend this? Knowing everything there is to know about me; yet, you chose me and you loved me. Where could I run so far that Your spirit would not be with me? If I ascend unto heaven or climb to a high spiritual plateau, You are there. If I make for myself a bed of hell here on this earth, destroyed by sins curse; You are still there with me. If I soar above the mountaintops high with wings of eagles or live in the deepest darkest trials of life; you are there to lead me through every step of my life and to hold me safe from even my own self destruction.

What an incredible thought!! Because I accepted the precious gift of salvation through His son, Jesus Christ—He will never leave me. In Psalms 37, He said, ²³The steps of a good man are ordered by the LORD: and he delighteth in his way.

: ²⁴Though he fall, he shall not be utterly cast down: for the LORD upholdeth him with his hand.
This is again expressed by Paul in Romans 8
³⁵Who shall separate us from the love of Christ? shall tribulation, or distress, or persecution, or famine, or nakedness, or peril, or sword?
³⁶As it is written, For thy sake we are killed all the day long; we are accounted as sheep for the slaughter.
³⁷Nay, in all these things we are more than conquerors through him that loved us.
³⁸For I am persuaded, that neither death, nor life, nor angels, nor principalities, nor powers, nor things present, nor things to come,
³⁹Nor height, nor depth, nor any other creature, shall be able to separate us from the love of God, which is in Christ Jesus our Lord.

In the worn edges of my Bible, I found myself writing; "not even my failures, my sorrows or me"

Neither do I have the right to stay and wallow in my guilt or my ineptness to getting it right. If I were to do that, then I would become useless in His work. Such unconditional love compels me to move forward, reaching for Him. Philippians 3 "¹³Brethren, I count not myself to have apprehended: but this one thing I do, <u>forgetting those things which are behind</u>, and reaching forth unto those things which are before,

¹⁴I press toward the mark for the prize of the high calling of God in Christ Jesus."

You see as long as God leaves me here on this earth, He still has a job for me to do. I cannot waste too much time beating myself up for all the failures of yesterday. He has a plan for my life. I must get about the business of restoration, so that I can do that work He wants and needs me to. I have so often fallen down during my life and there on the ground, I so often have been afraid to look up; but the truth is God is always standing there with His hands outstretched saying" Come on little girl, take my hand, I will lift you up touch your wounds and help on your way. We have things to do, come on, take my hand, my child we still have places to go." Beyond this, I do still cling to His promise in Romans 8: 28 "And we know that all things work together for good to them that love God, to them who are the called according to His purpose. 29 For whom He did foreknow, He also did predestinate to be conformed to the image of His Son, that he might be the first-born among many brethren."

I find it inconceivable at this moment to think I could ever look like Christ in my walk, in my actions and in my words; but He knows how. He knows exactly what it will take to transform me. He knows all of my frailties; still He chose me and He takes the responsibility of making me perfect not only in His sight by the blood of Christ, but in guiding all my down sittings and all my uprisings. His desire and ultimate goal is that I will look like Christ to a world that needs Him. He takes charge and responsibility for making this wayward drifter a vessel of beauty that pours forth the Glory of our Savior and King, Jesus Christ.

Some who read the introduction, might smugly think, "Well, I at least have not fallen as she did." Beware those are very similar to the words of Simon Peter before he betrayed Christ or I am certain David never believed he could have committed adultery or had a man murdered; yet, he did. Whatever is that sin which besets you; the steps for restoration that with God's help I hope to lay out for you and for me, will still ring true.

I do know that in this journey as a Christian, it has forever been true as is expressed in II Timothy 2:13 [13]If we believe not, yet he abideth faithful: he cannot deny himself" What a beautiful thought, when I am faithless, he is faithful. When my step falters or my faith is all gone, He remains faithful to me and continues right on loving me. He continues His work of transformation in me. Oh that I might be His faithful servant and never take my eyes off of Him again. His love, devotion and sacrifice demand no less of me.

What I must do is to take the focus off of me and place it on Him. If I continue to wallow in my guilt over my failure, once more I have failed to recognize that the only righteousness that counts with God is that which comes from Him. He is my righteousness. He paid the price that I might be righteous before God. He is the only righteousness in me. So the only way to live the Christian life is to constantly die to myself, that He might live through me. I must die to my desires so that He might express through me His desires. I must die to my petty complaining about circumstances and recognize that all my circumstances are sifted through His hands of love and would not occur in my life except He allowed it. Even the sifting of my faith by Satan occur only when He allows because He knows there are areas of chaff in my life that will interfere in my testimony for Him. He steadily weaves all the pieces of my life into a portrait of His son, Jesus Christ. This I declared through a poem I wrote a few years ago which has been made into a song.

The Master Weaver

Broken threads my life you found
And with your love each piece you bound
A song of love your lips resound
With gentle hands, each thread you place
Oh could it be, amazing grace
A picture clear, my Savior's face
What joy divine, could it be true
Each broken thread, you only knew
When woven tight would look like you

The Scarlet threads my broken heart
The deepest sorrows blue impart
Each silver thread of tears that fell

You guide my life with such detail
A brilliant gold, your love divine
My sins were washed, a white sublime
You gently weave with skillful hand
The portrait mine that you have planned

Oh, let me Lord remember this
That I might know with joy and bliss
You did ordain my every tear
That I might learn to never fear
That I might trust the weaver's hand
And on this hope and promise stand
Your love will always know what's best
Your cradling arms are where I rest

Broken threads my life you found
And with your love each piece you bound
A song of love your lips resound
With gentle hands, each thread you place
Oh could it be, amazing grace
A picture clear, my Savior's face
What joy divine, could it be true
Each broken thread, you only knew
When woven tight would look like you

CHAPTER 2

Man's Dilemma

Romans 7: ¹⁴For we know that the law is spiritual: but I am carnal, sold under sin.

¹⁵For that which I do I allow not: for what I would, that do I not; but what I hate, that do I.

¹⁶If then I do that which I would not, I consent unto the law that it is good.

¹⁷Now then it is no more I that do it, but sin that dwelleth in me.

¹⁸For I know that in me (that is, in my flesh,) dwelleth no good thing: for to will is present with me; but how to perform that which is good I find not.

¹⁹For the good that I would I do not: but the evil which I would not, that I do.

²⁰Now if I do that I would not, it is no more I that do it, but sin that dwelleth in me.

²¹I find then a law, that, when I would do good, evil is present with me.

²²For I delight in the law of God after the inward man:

²³But I see another law in my members, warring against the law of my

mind, and bringing me into captivity to the law of sin which is in my members.

²⁴O wretched man that I am! Who shall deliver me from the body of this death?

²⁵I thank God through Jesus Christ our Lord. So then with the mind I myself serve the law of God; but with the flesh the law of sin.

*W*hen we read these verses, most of us know that he is describing our own self. We struggle against the flesh and sin. At times, we want to just say, "Forget it" and give up. Still there is another voice inside for those of us who know Christ as our Savior—because He is living inside us and has given us the Holy Spirit to guide us and comfort us through these struggles. He is that still small voice that gently steadily draws us closer and closer to Him; that same voice that prays for us when we choose not to pray or draw aside from Him. He who knows what is best for me; despite, my total ignorance as to recognizing who He really is. Still for this chapter let me move forward and still attempt to explain this dilemma further and beg of you to not stop reading until you have read the next chapter which is God's answer. The worst place anyone can remain is in man's dilemma without knowing God's response. We need to gain an appreciation as to how truly unworthy we are and how ultimately worthy is Jesus Christ. We need to see how truly BIG He is and how truly small we are. We must also truly appreciate the utter importance of this spiritual war that we are in the center of. It is also imperative that we realize the beauty and intelligence of our arch enemy #1 Satan. Finally, we must understand what Satan's plan is.

When we look at our lives we tend to think way too much of ourselves. We think of ultimate importance our pain, our suffering, our tribulations, our loneliness and our wants. We continually come to God asking that He change our situation. It is not wrong to ask God about our needs or wants; but it is our attitude that this is all that is important. So often we moan and plead as though our very life and faith depend on His providing us with exactly what we want. So often we walk away and pout or even have a temper tantrum when He in His wisdom says "Child, that is not the best plan for you." When we are abused or have some chronic illness that day by day rips away at our body with pain, we cannot understand why a loving Father wouldn't immediately answer our request. We fail to accept that He is sovereign when we have suddenly lost everything due to a financial downfall. We either become like the two year old who pouts or we run straight to that lie "I knew it, He really doesn't love me." Within all this we see ourselves as way too important and see Him as too Little.

You see in this society in which we live so often we have our lives bombarded with the idea of the most important thing is our comfort and happiness. This gives us a misconception as to who God is. We tend to want Him to be only a Santa Claus God who is there to grant our every wish and remove every obstacle from our path. What a miniscule view of God and enormous view of our own importance here on this earth; as though, God is there to be our servant rather than we His. There are some who also believe that if you have accepted Christ as your Savior, you will automatically and forever more never make any major mistakes or commit any major sins. Again, with God sin is sin and we are the only ones who continue to justify ourselves by categorizing sin into major and minor. Perfect Righteousness cannot live with any unrighteousness whether it be that momentary jealous thought or that momentary lack of faith or that brief word that injured another's feelings or that little "righteous gossip so we might pray for that poor soul". All of these to God are sin as much so as murder, fornication, lascivious living or adultery. Others think that going to church more, tithing more, serving more and sacrificing more will improve your position with God. If you are doing these for that purpose instead of by allowing Him to do it through you then again you are wrong. The only righteousness that counts with God is the righteousness that comes from God.

If you ever want to fully understand the gospel of Jesus Christ and are prepared to spend hours in studying it; I urge you to begin an intense study of the book of Romans for therein lies the gospel broken down and explained by Paul as he wrote this letter by God's guiding hand to the Roman church who just didn't get it; as we don't most of the time. Paul quotes Old Testament scriptures when he wrote in Romans 3 [10]As it is written, There is none righteous, no, not one:

[11]There is none that understandeth, there is none that seeketh after God.

[12]They are all gone out of the way, they are together become unprofitable; there is none that doeth good, no, not one.

[13]Their throat is an open sepulchre; with their tongues they have used deceit; the poison of asps is under their lips:

[14]Whose mouth is full of cursing and bitterness:

[15]Their feet are swift to shed blood:

[16]Destruction and misery are in their ways:

[17]And the way of peace have they not known:

[18]There is no fear of God before their eyes.

[19]Now we know that what things soever the law saith, it saith to them who are under the law: that every mouth may be stopped, and the entire world may become guilty before God.

[20]Therefore by the deeds of the law there shall no flesh be justified in his sight: for by the law is the knowledge of sin.

And again in Romans 3:23 For all have sinned, and come short of the glory of God.

Those scriptures just shot down your excuse that "After all, I am not that bad. I have never been to jail, I don't beat my wife, I try to live as a good wife, I don't commit adultery," and on and on we go. Or even some, well after all I tithe, or I am a good person and help the poor, or I try to always treat my neighbors well. We continue on with look at all I have done or sacrificed for God, and we wait for a great reward. The keyword here is "I". It does not change the fact that ALL have sinned, and come SHORT of the Glory of God. Mankind may be able to exceed his own standards of good; but can never even come close to God's standards for righteousness. So often our sin is actually our putting ourselves in God's place and vainly attempting to work our way to being a "better person".

This is a heresy of our faith. As Paul described in Athens as recorded in Acts 17: [24]God that made the world and all things therein, seeing that he is Lord of heaven and earth, dwelleth not in temples made with hands;

[25]Neither is worshipped with men's hands, as though He needed any thing, seeing He giveth to all life, and breath, and all things;
[26]And hath made of one blood all nations of men for to dwell on all the face of the earth, and hath determined the times before appointed, and the bounds of their habitation;
[27]That they should seek the Lord, if haply they might feel after him, and find him, though he be not far from every one of us:
[28]For in Him we live, and move, and have our being; as certain also of your own poets have said, For we are also his offspring.

So it is, we see ourselves as too important and fail to see that "my life is not about me." He is the Creator and for that reason as His creation, He owns me. Everything is to bring Him glory and honor. He is sovereign, omniscient and has the best plan for each of His children.

Our second great problem is that we have such a small view of who God is. He is the Creator of the Universe and everything therein. The definition of the Universe is all matter and energy, including the earth, the galaxies, and the contents of intergalactic space, regarded as a whole. Therefore, He created me and has full dominion over my life. We see that in the scripture just presented above. When you gaze into the heavens on a star filled night imagine that God spoke each into being with one breath and knows each by name. David reminds us in "Psalms 8: [3]When I consider thy heavens, the work of thy fingers, the moon and the stars, which thou hast ordained; [4]What is man, that thou art mindful of him? and the son of man, that thou visitest him?" Or again in " Psalms 147 ³ He heals the brokenhearted and binds up their wounds. ⁴ He determines the number of the stars and calls them each by name. ⁵ Great is our Lord and mighty in power; his understanding has no limit." This verse also refers to His omnipotence which is defined as unlimited power, having unlimited authority or influence. He has unlimited power and unlimited authority to rule in our lives with the best that He has. Beyond that this same verse refers to the fact that He does this with His omniscience which can be defined as having infinite **awareness**, understanding, and insight. It is with this omnipotence, omniscience that He heals the brokenhearted and binds up their wounds. The Creator of the universe in His full knowledge and power knows what is best in my life and exactly what it will take to heal my sinful heart and draw me to Him. Beyond this He is omnipresent-that is He is present everywhere at the same time. The definition actually is present in all places at all times. That includes this moment, yesterday and infinitely into eternity He is present. **Sovereignty** is the quality of having supreme, independent authority over a territory. Because He is the omnipotent, omnipresent, omniscient Creator of the Universe, He has Sovereign rule over the Universe and over me. He has supreme rule over every detail of my life and He is there to mend my brokenness; then how can I ever doubt Him or His choices for my life. In our underestimation of Him, we also fail to recognize that we are created to bring Him Glory and anything that does not bring Him Glory is in contradiction to Him. Even those good things or charitable things that I do on my own to shine as my own Glory are in contradiction to Him. Beyond all this He is perfect Righteousness and perfect Justice. As perfect righteousness, He cannot accept less than perfect righteousness which I cannot achieve and therefore perfect justice must condemn me. To do anything less would then make Him not perfect in His justice. This creates a great gap between God and man which cannot be justified without the price for our sin being paid.

We underestimate God's righteousness and justice. We underestimate His wrath toward sin and by doing so we underestimate the price that

Christ paid-we trivialize His death and crucifixion in which He took God's wrath for us.

So we have already established the major dilemma, the first is that we are all sinful and unworthy of a relationship with a perfect, righteous God. This chasm must be bridged so that we can perform the one thing that we were designed to do and that is Glorify God. Yet there are some major struggles that we must deal with in order to serve Him and truly Glorify Him. The first of these is our refusal to see how insignificant we really are and the second is our failure to see God as He truly is and sovereign over this universe and each of our lives. Another great difficulty we have that presents another stumbling block is our inability or failure to see sin for what it really is.

Let me give you an example, which only those with pets might fully appreciate. One must be constantly vigilante in order to prevent a flea infestation. If not, they enter initially hidden and unnoticed, like that brief thought of doubt, anger or jealousy. Buried deep within the fur of your pet, they remain hidden until suddenly you realize that they have multiplied a million fold and have taken over your pet, your house. Sin is like that. It creeps in as a brief and fleeting thought hardly noticed which if left unchecked begins to multiply out of control, consuming our hope, our joy, and our faith.

"Romans 6: [23] For the wages of sin *is* death." So sin brings death. For those who do not accept Christ as their Savior, this is eternal death. Yet, for the Christian, sin still causes death—death to your testimony, death to your joy, death to that close communion with God, death to relationships, and death to all hope. "James 1: [14] But each one is tempted when he is drawn away by his own desires and enticed. [15] Then, when desire has conceived, it gives birth to sin; and sin, when it is full-grown, brings forth death." Again that tiny little hidden flea entering into our hearts through desires, then multiply and destroy. This can be sexual desire, the desire for power, the desire for money, the desire for prestige, or anything that we desire more than we desire God. It can be a desire even for what seems innocent. For me the desire for human love so

17

overwhelmed me at times that it clouded my path and allowed sin an entrance through wide open doors.

Another problem is our failure to see the magnitude of the spiritual battle in which we are engaged. So often we see the world through our stages and goals. Birth, first grade, high school, first love, college, first job, marriage, children and success seem to be the focus of this world. We become so focused on these fleeting moments of our life—which are mere moments compared to eternity. There is a spiritual battle that began before man ever was first formed. As we are told in Isaiah 14:

> [12] " How you are fallen from heaven,
> O Lucifer, son of the morning!
> *How* you are cut down to the ground,
> You who weakened the nations!
> [13] For you have said in your heart:
>
> ' I will ascend into heaven,
> I will exalt my throne above the stars of God;
> I will also sit on the mount of the congregation
> On the farthest sides of the north;
> [14] I will ascend above the heights of the clouds,
> I will be like the Most High.'
> [15] Yet you shall be brought down to Sheol,
> To the lowest depths of the Pit.
> [16] " Those who see you will gaze at you,
> *And* consider you, *saying:*
>
> ' *Is* this the man who made the earth tremble,
> Who shook kingdoms,
> [17] Who made the world as a wilderness
> And destroyed its cities,
> *Who* did not open the house of his prisoners?'

Thus, Satan fell from heaven and he is angry and bitter. He has one plan in mind and that is to take as many with him as he can. After all, in his anger he cannot accept that anyone worship or praise God—the object of his anger. We need to never underestimate him. He is described throughout the scripture as beautiful, intelligent and beguiling. As you will note in Ezekiel 28 where God speaks of His intelligence and His beauty while also telling him of his final destiny which is certain—for God is Sovereign and will complete this.

> 12" You *were* the seal of perfection,
> Full of wisdom and perfect in beauty.
> ¹³ You were in Eden, the garden of God;
> Every precious stone *was* your covering:
> The sardius, topaz, and diamond,
> Beryl, onyx, and jasper,
> Sapphire, turquoise, and emerald with gold.
> The workmanship of your timbrels and pipes
> Was prepared for you on the day you were created.
> ¹⁴ " You *were* the anointed cherub who covers;
> I established you;
> You were on the holy mountain of God;
> You walked back and forth in the midst of fiery stones.
> ¹⁵ You *were* perfect in your ways from the day you were created,
> Till iniquity was found in you.
> ¹⁶ " By the abundance of your trading
> You became filled with violence within,
> And you sinned;
> Therefore I cast you as a profane thing
> Out of the mountain of God;
> And I destroyed you, O covering cherub,
> From the midst of the fiery stones.
> ¹⁷ " Your heart was lifted up because of your beauty;
> You corrupted your wisdom for the sake of your splendor;

I cast you to the ground,
I laid you before kings,
That they might gaze at you.
[18] " You defiled your sanctuaries
By the multitude of your iniquities,
By the iniquity of your trading;
Therefore I brought fire from your midst;
It devoured you,
And I turned you to ashes upon the earth
In the sight of all who saw you.
[19] All who knew you among the peoples are astonished at you;
You have become a horror,
And *shall be* no more forever.""""

Do you get even a small idea of HOW BITTER SATAN IS.? He does not present himself as ugly holding a pitchfork so that we might see him. He is the great deceiver, murderer, tempter, destroyer, liar, accuser of the brethren, Prince of the world, roaring lion, and great imitator. Through beauty, charm, and knowledge of scripture he has infiltrated our churches, creating confusion. He knows that by drawing or charming anyone into any gospel that is anything except Christ Alone for salvation; then he will have cleverly prevented many from finding salvation. He also knows that the chaos and derision brought through religion will drive many away from seeking the Gospel of Christ. He is constantly seeking to destroy the testimony of the true followers of Christ, so as to silence their voices and make them appear as fools. "I Peter 5: [8]Be sober, be vigilant; because your adversary the devil, as a roaring lion, walketh about, seeking whom he may devour:" This warning was to the Christians.

We need to be ever aware of our purpose on this earth and quit moaning about such trivial things. Our entire lifetime, is but a second compared to eternity. We are in the center of the largest battlefield carrying across all the centuries. Our commander in chief is Jesus Christ whom we represent with every action of our lives. What we do for Christ is what matters. How much money I make, position I gain, cars I drive, or adoration I obtain won't matter much. All these possessions will fade into ruble like dust. What really matters is how many souls are pointed to Christ, how many eternities are changed because they were able to see Christ shining through my life. It changes the whole perspective of things if we see the urgency of this. We need to stop looking at all the petty things that bother us or that we think are important in our short sightedness and start making our decisions based on how will this affect my testimony for Christ—will it bring Him Glory.

But alas, back to the original dilemma—how do we accomplish this. Inside of me there is no good thing, so how can I ever get it right? I cannot do it on my own. I need a Savior to become my righteousness that I might be able to move forward in this my greatest purpose on earth. That is why God's plan of redemption is the only way this selfish heart can be transformed. If God did not provide an escape I would be forever condemned. As Isaiah 64:6 says But we are all as an unclean thing, and all our righteousnesses are as **filthy rags**; and we all do fade as a leaf; and our iniquities, like the wind, have taken us away."

EVIL SURROUNDS
Evil surrounds
Evil abounds
Pressing my life throughout each day
Quickening Sounds
Blaring around
Bidding my heart within to sway

Lord, let your light shine in my heart
Command all darkness to depart
Let Your love shine forth through me
That all evil is forced to flee

Evil Surrounds
Evil Abounds
Firm in Your Grace I cannot sway
Quickening Sounds
Blaring Around
Your still voice drives them away

It is Your love that presses on
When my strength is fully gone
Remove from me each selfish thought
On that cross my life You bought

Faith now Surounds
Hope now abounds
Your Righteousness gives way
Glorious Sounds
Praise all Around
Sin's chains are gone away

Let your love reach through these hands
Feet firm set on this grace in which I stand
Let your glory shine through me
A light a darkened world might see.

CHAPTER 3

God's Answer to Man's Sin

Ephesians 2

[1]And you hath he quickened, who were dead in trespasses and sins;

[2]Wherein in time past ye walked according to the course of this world, according to the prince of the power of the air, the spirit that now worketh in the children of disobedience:

[3]Among whom also we all had our conversation in times past in the lusts of our flesh, fulfilling the desires of the flesh and of the mind; and were by nature the children of wrath, even as others.

[4]But God, who is rich in mercy, for his great love wherewith he loved us,

[5]Even when we were dead in sins, hath quickened us together with Christ, (by grace ye are saved;)

[6]And hath raised us up together, and made us sit together in heavenly places in Christ Jesus:

[7]That in the ages to come he might shew the exceeding riches of his grace in his kindness toward us through Christ Jesus.

[8]For by grace are ye saved through faith; and that not of yourselves: it is the gift of God:

[9]Not of works, lest any man should boast.

¹⁰For we are his workmanship, created in Christ Jesus unto good works, which God hath before ordained that we should walk in them.

I need righteousness to be acceptable to God-but what I have is sin, which God hates and His justice demands payment. He cannot change His character to get around this. His wrath flames hot against all sin. His perfect righteousness, omniscience and sovereignty see beyond our pretences reaching deep into the hidden recesses of our hearts and knows every evil thought that may pass our minds. Yet, His love for mankind was so great that He provided a plan for redemption, the only plan acceptable. He knew that His plan would send His Son to suffer beyond anything that we can imagine and at the same time would also fully Glorify His Son. This was never a last minute thought or an "oops, what are we going to do." So, knowing that Adam would sin, He already had the plan for redemption. Somewhat, the same as He has for each of my sins; He already has the out—but that is another story.

Some would like to say that if God is truly merciful; then He would just pardon everyone and it wouldn't matter. Surely if God is truly a loving God then He would not send anyone to Hell; all of us will make it somehow. Nothing could be so far from the truth. Although no earthly example can fully demonstrate this I want to attempt to raise a little emotion toward understanding and grasping this.

One day while at home with your son, another breaks in ties you up and before your eyes sodomizes, tortures, and kills your son. You realize that this is the same person who had been rejecting and tormenting your son for all his life. He is then brought to trial and convicted to be sentenced to death; but wait, the judge decides to be merciful and just let him go with no-one paying the price. Most likely you would be outraged beyond any emotion that could even be imagined. You would demand justice—someone must pay the price. Whatever thread of righteousness you hold within your heart would reach out and demand Justice be done and in fact you would most likely take matters into your own hands and kill the intruder. Justice demands it. What if you then find out that your son chose to be the one to suffer so as to save the life of another little boy who had spit on him every day at school? Would you then immortalize your son as a hero worthy of praise and honor? What if the judge sends his own son to pay the price of the intruder? What a waste unless there is a change in the heart of the intruder. The intruder needs a change of heart, a righteousness not his own. So if the judge's innocent son dies to pay the price and offers to the intruder as a gift the righteous heart that had been the child's. Would not the intruder be obligated by sheer love to do everything to honor, adore and glorify this child? But to do it only out of love and adoration still does not get it right; because tomorrow the true nature of the intruder will battle against the new nature unless somehow the giver can impart truly a new nature that is able to transform the heart of the intruder and promises his spirit to abide with the intruder to guide him in that transformation.

If you say, but I never harmed Christ in any way; then, you still fail to understand the magnitude of sin and fail to see the magnitude of Glory which is Gods. This leap of truth is so difficult I fear I have no words to help you cross it and only pray that God illuminate it for you. 2 Corinthians 4 "³But if our gospel be hid, it is hid to them that are lost: ⁴In whom the god of this world hath blinded the minds of them which believe not, lest the light of the glorious gospel of Christ, who is the image of God, should shine unto them. ⁵For we preach not ourselves, but Christ Jesus the Lord; and ourselves your servants for Jesus' sake. ⁶For God, who commanded the light to shine out of darkness, hath shined in our hearts, to give the light of the knowledge of the glory of God in the face of Jesus Christ." Before you can even begin to understand the depths of what Christ did for you on the cross; you must first understand the depths of sin that resides lurking in your depraved heart. Until you fully comprehend that every one of us on our own are deserving of only the full wrath of this Omnipotent, Sovereign, Almighty God; you cannot appreciate the magnificence of Glory that was displayed by Christ as He Willingly Suffered and Died to pay the price that justice demanded.

It is not enough to merely have our sins paid for because we need perfect righteousness to commune with and be acceptable to God. The only righteousness that is acceptable to God is that which comes from God. Romans 3: "[11]There is none that understandeth, there is none that seeketh after God. [12]They are all gone out of the way, they are together become unprofitable; there is none that doeth good, no, not one. [13]Their throat is an open sepulchre; with their tongues they have used deceit; the poison of asps is under their lips:"Thus we are in desperate need of the Great Exchange offered by Christ—I give Him my sin and He gives me His righteousness. If I understand this, then I must see Him as ultimately worthy of my praise. I must see Him with the eyes of my heart in all His splendor and beauty, so worthy of my praise that even if He gave me nothing in return, even if salvation were not on the table, He would be worthy of my praise. As I plead this, I also say a whispered prayer as did Paul the Apostle in Ephesians 1 "[17]That the God of our Lord Jesus Christ, the Father of glory, may give unto you the spirit of wisdom and revelation in the knowledge of him: [18]The eyes of your understanding being enlightened; that ye may know what is the hope of his calling, and what the riches of the glory of his inheritance in the saints, [19]And what is the exceeding greatness of his power to us-ward who believe, according to the working of his mighty power, [20]Which he wrought in Christ, when he raised him from the dead, and set him at his own right hand in the heavenly places, [21]Far above all principality, and power, and might, and dominion, and every name that is named, not only in this world, but also in that which is to come: [22]And hath put all things under his feet, and gave him to be the head over all things to the church, [23]Which is his body, the fulness of him that filleth all in all"

That would be more than I could ever deserve or hope for; yet, that is not all He has given to me at the point of my seeing Him in all His glory, seeing me in all my guilt and suddenly, miraculously falling so in love with Him that I must follow Him wherever He leads. At that moment, I am saved. He then richly makes me a joint-heir of all that He has. Romans 8: "¹⁴For as many as are led by the Spirit of God, they are the sons of God. " ¹⁵For ye have not received the spirit of bondage again to fear; but ye have received the Spirit of adoption, whereby we cry, Abba, Father. ¹⁶The Spirit itself beareth witness with our spirit, that we are the children of God: ¹⁷And if children, then heirs; heirs of God, and joint-heirs with Christ; if so be that we suffer with him, that we may be also glorified together." We are given this assurance by Christ Himself that the Holy Spirit will be there within us to help us in all our infirmities, John 14: "¹⁵If ye love me, keep my commandments. ¹⁶And I will pray the Father, and he shall give you another Comforter, that he may abide with you **for ever;** ¹⁷Even the Spirit of truth; whom the world cannot receive, because it seeth him not, neither knoweth him: but ye know him; for he dwelleth with you, and shall be in you." So, I do love you Lord, what are your commandments? Mark 8: "³⁴And when he had called the people unto him with his disciples also, he said unto them, Whosoever will come after me, let him deny himself, and take up his cross, and follow me." Ok, so does this bring me back to works? No, never, it is a statement to explain what the necessary degree of love and adoration to follow Him is.

Again I need divine help for you to understand this because of my own inadequacy of explaining. Salvation is not saying, "Ok, I really do not want to go to hell and that thing about receiving something from Him, maybe take care of my problems—that sounds good. I guess I can start going to church and maybe even sing in the choir. After all, I guess that is a pretty good bargain." Maybe I need to give you an example, I have worked in a jail ministry and it is amazing to see how many come to the Bible study and pray a quoted prayer of salvation; but come for only one thing—they want God to set them free from jail. Greater than 75% throw away the Bible as they walk out the door. Some only want the financial help, housing and clothing they can get from the church; but are not really seeing, savoring, and seeking this worthy King. These usually fall by the wayside when the gifts of the people begin to diminish. It is my fear that there are many such sinners filling our church pews—what a sad thought. This is not only among those who have been imprisoned in a jail; but also to so many who are imprisoned in their lives of seeming affluence or a prison of their own selfish ambition. So many are seeking the gift but not the giver and thus even our churches and pulpits may be filled with unbelievers. So my first question of you is, "Do you know Him as your Lord and Savior?"

He also gave us the promise that He would perform the work of keeping us. John 6 " [37]All that the Father giveth me shall come to me; and him that cometh to me I will in no wise cast out. [38]For I came down from heaven, not to do mine own will, but the will of him that sent me. [39]And this is the Father's will which hath sent me, that of all which he hath given me I should lose nothing, but should raise it up again at the last day. [40]And this is the will of him that sent me, that every one which seeth the Son, and believeth on him, may have everlasting life: and I will raise him up at the last day." Psalm 37: "[23]The steps of a good man are ordered by the LORD: and he delighteth in his way. [24]Though he fall, he shall not be utterly cast down: for the LORD upholdeth him with his hand. [25]I have been young, and now am old; yet have I not seen the righteous forsaken, nor his seed begging bread." This is further demonstrated in the scriptures of Paul where he wrote in Romans 8 "[35]Who shall separate us from the love of Christ? shall tribulation, or distress, or persecution, or famine, or nakedness, or peril, or sword? [36]As it is written, For thy sake we are killed all the day long; we are accounted as sheep for the slaughter. [37]Nay, in all these things we are more than conquerors through him that loved us. [38]For I am persuaded, that neither death, nor life, nor angels, nor principalities, nor powers, nor things present, nor things to come, [39]Nor height, nor depth, nor any other creature, shall be able to separate us from the love of God, which is in Christ Jesus our Lord" He has promised to never let us go once we are His. In the recesses of my Bible during various moments in my life I have written not even my depression, my failure, nor I can keep me from His love. What an incredible promise!!!.

Still that is not all He has promised. He promises to perfect me and make me look like Christ. In fact, He has determined that I will share in His Glory, as will everyone who has accepted Him as Lord and Savior. The very thought of that is too great for me. Romans 8: " [29]For whom he did foreknow, he also did predestinate to be conformed to the image of his Son, that he might be the firstborn among many brethren. [30]Moreover whom he did predestinate, them he also called: and whom he called, them he also justified: and whom he justified, them he also glorified." This is again reiterated in II Corinthians 3: "[18]But we all, with open face beholding as in a glass the glory of the Lord, are changed into the same image from glory to glory, even as by the Spirit of the Lord" It is His work to perfect us, transform us, and make us look like Jesus in spirit and action so that we may carry out His commission to go out and tell a dying world of Jesus Christ, the only living bread. Philippians 1: "Being confident of this very thing, that he which hath begun a good work in you will perform it until the day of Jesus Christ"

Do you truly believe that? Actually that is precisely where the problem lies a lot of the time. God has promised us not just salvation from the punishment from sin and a hope in heaven one day; but He also promised us His righteousness, His power, His strength, and His presence to walk with us every step of the way. He has promised to transform us and complete the work He began. We seem to accept that He may purchase our salvation; but to change this heart—well I better do that to prove to Him that I am worthy or to pay a debt. I may have the faith that He saved me or that He provided for yesterday's grace; but do I truly believe Him to be the finisher of my faith as well? Do I trust Him for tomorrow's grace? Do I really believe that everything that comes into my life comes sifted through His Mighty Hands of Love? A big part in my failing to get it right has come directly as a result of my lack of faith in Future Grace. I do not believe He can do it, so I try to do it myself and fail every time either by the act of failing or by the heart of pride with which I have performed the work. Unless it is His Heart performing the work through me then it is futile.

This does not mean that I run after sin and say, "Oh, well, He will take care of it one day." I pray tell that could only be said by someone who does not know Him. If He lives in your heart, you may not be winning the battles; but you will still be battling against sin. His love demands it. The shear knowledge that you grieve Him would be more than you could bear. But what I am saying is that the way to battle Satan is by faith in God's words and by using God's own words back to Satan. To do that, I must grow in the knowledge of Him and His word. I will not find Him by chasing parties or entertainment or TV. I must see Him as more important than anything else. If I become nonchalant about this or ignore Him, He knows how to get my attention again; because He knows that the only way I can truly be joyful and peaceful is when I am close to Him. Yet, God in His Marvelous mercy and grace provided us with much more to assist the justified Christian in his journey here on this earth. He gave us His word to guide us. He left His love letters to guide His children. It is by searching and reading His words that we may come to know Him in His full glory and majesty and there is where we grow more in love with Him each day. As we grow more in love with Him, the more we long to hear His voice and to spend time alone with Him.

What a wondrous plan He devised to solve man's dilemma. He has provided us with everything we need to commune with Him. He paid the price for my sin so that I could be His child and thereby find the strength, joy and hope for this journey while awaiting that precious moment that He calls me home into His presence.

Glory to Glory

Glory to Glory, my life now defined
Boughten, redeemed by Your love divine
Transforming my life by Your joy sublime
Laying my life down, I give you my time
To seek your full Glory, all else I resign.

Undeserving I be, now my sins You erase
Let me lay down my life for my cross to embrace
What else could I seek but Your glorious face
Right there beside me each step of this race
It is Your joy, Your peace, Your mercy, Your grace

CHAPTER 4

Why Do Christians Suffer?

II Corinthians 4: ¹Therefore seeing we have this ministry, as we have received mercy, we faint not; ²But have renounced the hidden things of dishonesty, not walking in craftiness, nor handling the word of God deceitfully; but by manifestation of the truth commending ourselves to every man's conscience in the sight of God. ³But if our gospel be hid, it is hid to them that are lost: ⁴In whom the god of this world hath blinded the minds of them which believe not, lest the light of the glorious gospel of Christ, who is the image of God, should shine unto them. ⁵For we preach not ourselves, but Christ Jesus the Lord; and ourselves your servants for Jesus' sake. ⁶For God, who commanded the light to shine out of darkness, hath shined in our hearts, to give the light of the knowledge of the glory of God in the face of Jesus Christ. ⁷But we have this treasure in earthen vessels, that the excellency of the power may be of God, and not of us. ⁸We are troubled on every side, yet not distressed; we are perplexed, but not in despair; ⁹Persecuted, but not forsaken; cast down, but not destroyed; ¹⁰Always bearing about in the body the dying of the Lord Jesus, that the life also of Jesus might be made manifest in our body. ¹¹For we which live are always delivered unto death for Jesus' sake, that the life also of Jesus might be made manifest in our mortal flesh. [12]So then death worketh in us, but life in you.

The question of suffering in the life of the Christian has probably had more volumes written than many subjects. Yet, there is no volume of work greater than that of the Holy Bible itself that declares the purposes of pain and suffering. Suffering comes in so many forms and varies with each individual. For some the sheer worry that they might be late to an appointment becomes so intense as to cause great emotional distress. For another, they may be living with chronic pain and physical suffering. Another may have been born with an emotional illness so intense as to interfere with their ability to ever experience joy. Some have been subjected to intense abuse both physical and mental. In another instance, one may be facing severe ridicule due to their economic or physical differences. Yet, there is one common thread that on this earth at some time and to some degree, everyone will at some point suffer loss, pain and tribulations. There are some who want to teach that once a Christian, all these circumstances of pain or illness can be completely cured by prayers of deep faith. Some would try to say that any suffering or trial in a Christians life comes as a result of either sin or a lack of faith; thus returning us all to the law for blessings. This is a complete heresy as God's word takes a completely different view of trials and tribulations. The studying of God's word regarding suffering and trials has taken up a great deal of my lifetime while I have tried to find and make sense of my own life. Pain and suffering have always been a very real part of my life. Included among my certificates are emotional abuse, physical abuse, cancer, financial disasters, chronic illness, multiple abdominal surgeries, widowhood, sense of inadequacy, and a sense of loneliness. This has been a very long journey of learning step by step about God's view of suffering and what my role is. Most recently, I had a complete abdominal wall reconstruction due to multiple hernias with intermittent episodes of obstruction inflicting acute pain. The surgery has proven to be one of the most painful for recovery with my lying at moments with such severe muscle spasm as to be unable to move so that tears would be sliding down my cheeks despite my attempts to be brave. I, who prided myself in the ability to tolerate high levels of pain and never take pain medications, was literally brought to my knees and am still 2 weeks out unable to lift even so much as a picture of water. For the first time in my life I am forced to continue pain meds beyond the first week and one half. Perhaps God wanted to force me to sit down to finish this book writing assignment He gave me a while back.

As I lay in the bed at the hospital during two separate occasions last week, I was left with no IV access and no pain meds. I remember then and on other occasions while lying there that I looked into heaven and cried "God, why so much pain? I know that this is part of your will and plan for my life, but why? What need I learn? Was my pride in the way? Is there someone I need to tell about you, give me strength to testify Your Glory even while hurting so. The greatest part of the pain wrapped around my ribcage involving the lowest ribs to which multiple stitches had been placed. When the pain was nearly unbearable at one point, I suddenly realized that this pain was nothing compared to the pain that Christ felt after He had been beaten and the flesh torn from all His ribs. I suddenly saw His pain in a new light. The world believes it a strange thought, that a God of perfect love would desire us to suffer such pain and trials; after all, did He not promise joy, peace and rest in Him. Therein lies the great mystery and the wonder of the Christian life and the answer forevermore to the mighty question "Why do Christians suffer?" It is the question that burns in the mind of every believer at some moment or time. Still, it is there that we come to find who God truly is and the majesty of His heart of love for each and every one of us. It is our testimony to the remainder of the world which is lost and dying. It is the heart and the soul of the gospel of Christ. From the center of this brokenness, God can demonstrate His greatest power and love. It is in the depth of this understanding and coming to the very end of one's self that He is able to fill us with His fullness that a world might see Him shine through us. It is there that we reach the depth and the understanding of His broken heart for a dying world. It is when we begin to see our pain and sorrow through the eyes of a loving God that we may truly understand and say "Thank you, Lord for these my tears which draw me closer ever to thee." When you see a gentle, kind woman whose dreams have all been broken who reaches out to help others to fly, you stand in wonder and awe. A world looking on begins to wonder what it is that she has that gives her strength and long to have the same. It is that wonder which draws others to Christ himself. After all, He gave up the majesty of His throne to come to the earth and suffer hunger, pain, sorrow, betrayal and death that we might be saved. Would our walk on this earth to become more like Him demand any less? When we reach the point that we understand that every minute detail of our life as a Christian is sifted through God's hand of love, only then can we truly grow through each painful process and become the beautiful vessel God intended us to be. Only then can we "mount up with wings as eagles".

I contend that there are six major reasons for pain in our lives. 1. We live in a fallen world. 2. As a direct consequence of our own willful sin (not a punishment merely a direct reaction for our action) 3. To turn us around from a dangerous path which will lead to our destruction. 4. To grow us up. 5. For the good of the kingdom. 6. To develop intimacy with Christ. These are the six reasons God allows or even brings sometimes the suffering into our lives.

These points are demonstrated throughout the Bible in the lives of God's men and women. So often in Christianity we want to preach a gospel of prosperity because we think that this would appeal to the crowds. So many sects attempt to teach this and have hoards of followers walking down the path to final destruction. This is the gospel that Satan would want us to hear; yet, it is not the gospel of Christ. You might say that if that be the case you don't want to hear anymore about the gospel; yet, let me assure you that having walked this very journey of pain and suffering I would do it all again and cry every tear again for the magnificent glory of knowing Christ. My heart is filled with joy beyond measure and a peace unshakable by earthly sorrows because of this great and mighty knowledge of Him. Only when I came to the end of myself could I be filled with His joy, His peace, His wonder and His power. Yet, with me this remains God's work in progress because despite all that I have been taught; there are moments while in this human body I look away and lose sight for a moment. Yet, those moments become fewer with time and I awaken each morning with the excited expectation of waiting to see what wondrous gift He has in store for me today.

Within the body of God's love letters to us, He has provided many examples to further support my position of the six reasons that God allows and even brings sorrow into our lives. That is what I hope to bring to light in your lives through this chapter of this book. Once you are able to see your sorrows and trials through the eyes of God, the burden lightens and you become able to say "Thank you, Lord, for I know your hand is in this and there is somewhere within this sorrow a gift of love from you." The truth is for each child of God, everything that happens in our life is sifted through God's mighty hands of love; therefore, EVERYTHING that occurs in our life is a GIFT OF LOVE from an almighty, all-knowing, loving heavenly Father. Once you see this and understand it, your entire life becomes transformed into a fountain of hope, inspiration and peace.

It is learning to see our lives through the eyes of God Himself. Much of what is frustration, pain and sorrow comes from a misguided expectation of what we "deserve". Unfortunately we are mistakenly taught to believe it is our right to have comfort, health, possessions, and worldly happiness. Therefore, many come to believe and even teach a "Santa Claus God". Yet, God knows that happiness, peace and joy only results from a deep relationship with Him. That place of true joy and peace comes only from understanding who He is. Nothing else, nor any other relationship can fulfill our desires or needs the way He can.

The Bible says in Romans 8: 28And we know that all things work together for good to them that love God, to them who are the called according to his purpose. **29For whom he did foreknow, he also did predestinate to be conformed to the image of his Son,** that he might be the firstborn among many brethren. How can I ever look like Christ if I have never carried a cross? There is a compassion and love that can come from a walk with sorrow which is unable to be found anywhere else.

We do live in a fallen world where evil does exist and Satan would like nothing better than to replace joyfulness with puckered faces, like a plum with all the water of life extracted resulting in that prune faced look. In this he seems to have a large following of grumbling, unhappy so called Christians who would not be able to draw anyone toward the light. More than this he loves to confuse the gospel of Christ by mingling truth with falsehood in addition to creating multiple religions which battle and fight against each other rather than to concentrate on teaching the gospel of Christ. There are also the changes in nature secondary to the fall which results in ever increasing illness and devastation. There is the greed of mankind's heart that leads to the destruction of nature and to financial turmoil throughout the world. Some of the suffering in this world is a direct result of this and also a means for us to be able to recognize and be reminded of the true state of affairs in which we live. The evil surrounding us gives us the first glimpse into the state of mankind, his separation from His creator and purpose, and the need of a Savior. Psalm 19: "¹The heavens declare the glory of God; and the firmament sheweth his handywork. ²Day unto day uttereth speech, and night unto night sheweth knowledge. ³There is no speech nor language, where their voice is not heard. ⁴Their line is gone out through all the earth, and their words to the end of the world. In them hath he set a tabernacle for the sun, ⁵Which is as a bridegroom coming out of his chamber, and rejoiceth as a strong man to run a race. ⁶His going forth is from the end of the heaven, and his circuit unto the ends of it: and there is nothing hid from the heat thereof. ⁷The law of the LORD is perfect, converting the soul: the testimony of the LORD is sure, making wise the simple. ⁸The statutes of the LORD are right, rejoicing the heart: the commandment of the LORD is pure, enlightening the eyes.

Everything around us reminds us of a Sovereign God for whom we need communion with and the law itself reminds us that we cannot reach Him of our own accord. Romans 3: ¹⁰As it is written, There is none righteous, no, not one: ¹¹There is none that understandeth, there is none that seeketh after God. ¹²They are all gone out of the way, they are together become unprofitable; there is none that doeth good, no, not one. ¹³Their throat is an open sepulchre; with their tongues they have used deceit; the poison of asps is under their lips: ¹⁴Whose mouth is full of cursing and bitterness: ¹⁵Their feet are swift to shed blood: ¹⁶Destruction and misery are in their ways: ¹⁷And the way of peace have they not known: ¹⁸There is no fear of God before their eyes. ¹⁹**Now we know that what things soever the law saith, it saith to them who are under the law: that every mouth may be stopped, and all the world may become guilty before God.** ²⁰Therefore by the deeds of the law there shall no flesh be justified in his sight: **for by the law is the knowledge of sin.**

A second reason for pain and suffering is similar in that there are some direct consequences to certain actions. For example, smoking increases a person's chances of lung cancer; therefore, if you smoke and get lung cancer it is a direct consequence not a direct punishment by God for the lack of care of the temple given. Promiscuous relationships may lead to HIV or Syphilis which can be a direct consequence of the action of promiscuity. If you yell at your boss, you might just find yourself without a job. In these circumstances, the problem is that generally guilt and condemnation become such a part of the person's response to the trial that it adds an unnecessary burden and weight to the trial and many times prevents the person from focusing on "what does God have for me in this trial?" Sometimes in these cases there is a sense that you cannot even bring this to Christ's feet because of recurrent sin. Yet, for the one who knows Christ as their Savior this is not true. Will God remove the consequence? Maybe, Maybe not; but He will walk through it with you. Let me give you a few scriptures to help you deal with the guilt if that is your case. Primarily remember that salvation is by grace alone through Christ alone. Romans 8: ¹There is therefore now no condemnation to them which are in Christ Jesus, who walk not after the flesh, but after the Spirit. ²For the law of the Spirit of life in Christ Jesus hath made me free from the law of sin and death. .. ⁹But ye are not in the flesh, but in the Spirit, if so be that the Spirit of God dwell in you." So if you know Christ as your Savior, then you know that the Holy Spirit Dwells within you, and there is therefore (because of clause a and b) no condemnation. When we wallow in self condemnation with guilt laden hearts we have taken our eyes off of Christ in all His Glory and refocused our attention on ourselves somehow believing that we had something to do with our salvation and sanctification to begin with. Guilt will not be able to make you more holy, so you must take your eyes off of you and refocus on Christ Himself. Phillippians 3: " Brethren, I count not myself to have apprehended: but this one thing I do, **forgetting** those things which are **behind**, and reaching forth unto those things which are before, I press toward the mark for the prize of the high calling of God in Christ Jesus." It is difficult not to dwell on our own failures which may have added to the current trial; but, we are commanded not to dwell. We press forward focusing on the author and finisher of our faith.

A third reason that trials come into our lives is that God needs to get our attention to turn us around from a dangerous path which will lead to our destruction. Sometimes in this Christian walk we are very much like sheep who wander about through the meadows not even noticing that we are approaching a dangerous area. Sometimes we become complacent in the routines of our daily life, giving little notice to the Bible lying beside our bed. Maybe not in particular looking to go the wrong direction; yet, ending up down some dead-end street going to nowhere. Or perhaps you saw all the warning signs and all the danger signs; still, choosing to go down the wrong path for whatever excuse you could make up. Just like the shepherd might need to use his staff to redirect the sheep; God, needs to get our attention and get us to turn around. Hebrews 12: ⁵And ye have forgotten the exhortation which speaketh unto you as unto children, My son, despise not thou the chastening of the Lord, nor faint when thou art rebuked of him: ⁶For whom the Lord loveth he chasteneth, and scourgeth every son whom he receiveth. ⁷If ye endure chastening, God dealeth with you as with sons; for what son is he whom the father chasteneth not?" This is a rod that is not meant to have us "pay for your sins"; but, rather a nudging to get us turned around and pointed in the right direction. When facing this kind of a trial, it is good to remember Psalm 23: ¹The LORD is my shepherd; I shall not want. ²He maketh me to lie down in green pastures: he leadeth me beside the still waters. ³He restoreth my soul: he leadeth me in the paths of righteousness for his name's sake. ⁴Yea, though I walk through the valley of the shadow of death, I will fear no evil: for thou art with me; thy rod and thy staff they comfort me." We too often fail to see the rod and staff as comforting; however, the truth is they are a reminder of His love which cannot allow us to wander off into dangerous paths. Instead "He leadeth me in the paths of righteousness."

A fourth reason for pain and tribulation to come into our lives is to grow us up. Before a baby can walk, they must first learn to crawl and then venture out on wobbly limbs with a few falls and scrapes before mastering the ability. We in our Christian walk are very similar. Throughout the scripture, God assures us that He is taking the responsibility of finishing the work of growing us up into the image of Jesus Christ. Who is better suited for the task of transforming me than an Omniscient, Sovereign, and Omnipotent Creator. After all, He formed me in my mother's womb and knows everything about me yesterday, today and tomorrow. As the master potter, He is the one who knows just how much pain, sorrow, stretching, failures are needed to change me into an image of Jesus Christ. A few verses to remind you of this being His primary work. Romans 8: "²⁹"For whom he did foreknow, he also did predestinate to be conformed to the image of his

Son; "Phillippians 1: " ⁶Being confident of this very thing, that he which hath begun a good work in you will perform it until the day of Jesus Christ:" II Corinthians 3: ¹⁸"But we all, with open face beholding as in a glass the glory of the Lord, are changed into the same image from glory to glory, even as by the Spirit of the Lord" Wow, actually I am so glad that He takes the responsibility of the work of changing me; as I would not have a clue how to transform me. This change may require a lot of refining—I Peter 1: ⁷"That the trial of your faith, being much more precious than of gold that perisheth, though it be tried with fire, might be found unto praise and honour and glory at the appearing of Jesus Christ:" He is changing us just as a potter forming the clay, as noted in Isaiah 64: 8 "But now, O LORD, thou art our father; we are the clay, and thou our **potter**; and we all are the work of thy hand." Romans 9: ²⁰"Nay but, O man, who art thou that repliest against God? Shall the thing formed say to him that formed it, Why hast thou made me thus? ²¹Hath not the potter power over the clay, of the same lump to make one vessel unto honour, and another unto dishonour? ²²What if God, willing to shew his wrath, and to make his power known, endured with much longsuffering the vessels of wrath fitted to destruction" As, He has chosen me to be His child how then can I ever complain as to the method it takes to make me a vessel of beauty for His glory?

A fifth reason for pain and suffering in the life of a Christian is for the Good of the Kingdom. It is many times necessary for the work of Christ to continue that His followers must endure great pain, sorrow and tribulation. Perhaps this is best illustrated by two simple stories chosen out of the hundreds lining the scripture. Stephen was chosen for his great faith to take a position of ministry in the early church. Acts 6: ⁸"And Stephen, full of faith and power, did great wonders and miracles among the people.. ¹⁰And they were not able to resist the wisdom and the spirit by which he spake. ¹¹Then they suborned men, which said, We have heard him speak blasphemous words against Moses, and against God. ¹²And they stirred up the people, and the elders, and the scribes, and came upon him, and caught him, and brought him to the council,

¹³And set up false witnesses, which said, This man ceaseth not to speak blasphemous words against this holy place, and the law: ¹⁴For we have heard him say, that this Jesus of Nazareth shall destroy this place, and shall change the customs which Moses delivered us. ¹⁵And all that sat in the council, looking stedfastly on him, saw his face as it had been the face of an angel" He continued to preach the truth, for which he was stoned—As the story is told Acts 7: ⁵⁵But he, being full of the Holy Ghost, looked up stedfastly into heaven, and saw the glory of God, and Jesus standing on the right hand of God, ⁵⁶And said, Behold, I see the heavens opened, and the Son of man standing on the right hand of God. ⁵⁷Then they cried out with a loud voice, and stopped their ears, and ran upon him with one accord, ⁵⁸And cast him out of the city, and stoned him: and the witnesses laid down their clothes at a young man's feet, whose name was Saul. ⁵⁹And they stoned Stephen, calling upon God, and saying, Lord Jesus, receive my spirit. ⁶⁰And he kneeled down, and cried with a loud voice, Lord, lay not this sin to their charge. And when he had said this, he fell asleep." Tragedy!! yes in our eyes; but God had a bigger plan for the kingdom and as noted He was there with Stephen each step of the way. How often do missionaries die in the work of Christ? How often is our pain and suffering there only so that we might point toward His Glory in the center of our suffering. It is commonplace to see people appear happy in prosperity; however, the true joy we have seen in the saintly Christians laidened with suffering and yet a powerful testimony for Christ Jesus—they change our lives. The second biblical life I want to exemplify to further explain this phenomenon is that of Paul the Apostle. We just met him in the previous scripture about Stephen; as it was he (Saul) that ordered the murder of Stephen and the clothes were laid at his feet. He watched as this saintly young preacher died praising his Lord and asking forgiveness for his murderers. Did this sight of Stephen's death play a role in the salvation of Paul? I daresay it must have played a part in the preparation of a wayward, stony heart. Did this sight haunt him later, a reminder of how great was God's grace in his salvation? Yet, after his salvation,

Paul became one of the greatest teachers of the faith. Perhaps, what he saw in Stephen affected his willingness to sacrifice himself for the sake of the gospel. Perhaps this is why Paul would be able to write in 2 Corinthians 11: [23]"Are they ministers of Christ? (I speak as a fool) I am more; in labours more abundant, in stripes above measure, in prisons more frequent, in deaths oft. [24]Of the Jews five times received I forty stripes save one. [25]Thrice was I beaten with rods, once was I stoned, thrice I suffered shipwreck, a night and a day I have been in the deep; [26]In journeyings often, in perils of waters, in perils of robbers, in perils by mine own countrymen, in perils by the heathen, in perils in the city, in perils in the wilderness, in perils in the sea, in perils among false brethren; [27]In weariness and painfulness, in watchings often, in hunger and thirst, in fastings often, in cold and nakedness. [28]Beside those things that are without, that which cometh upon me daily, the care of all the churches. [29]Who is weak, and I am not weak? who is offended, and I burn not? [30]If I must needs glory, I will glory of the things which concern mine infirmities. [31]The God and Father of our Lord Jesus Christ, which is blessed for evermore, knoweth that I lie not. [32]In Damascus the governor under Aretas the king kept the city of the damascenes with a garrison, desirous to apprehend me: [33]And through a window in a basket was I let down by the wall, and escaped his hands". Yet despite this degree of suffering, He exhorted us to live this same example of faith. In 2 Corinthians 6 he wrote, "[1]We then, as workers together with him, beseech you also that ye receive not the grace of God in vain. [2](For he saith, I have heard thee in a time accepted, and in the day of salvation have I succoured thee: behold, now is the accepted time; behold, now is the day of salvation.) [3]Giving no offence in any thing, that the ministry be not blamed: [4]But in all things approving ourselves as the ministers of God, in much patience, in afflictions, in necessities, in distresses, [5]In stripes, in imprisonments, in tumults, in labours, in watchings, in fastings; [6]By pureness, by knowledge, by long suffering, by kindness, by the Holy Ghost, by love unfeigned, [7]By the word of truth, by the power of God, by the armour of righteousness on the right hand and on the left, [8]By honour and dishonour, by evil report and good report: as deceivers, and yet true; [9]As unknown, and yet well known; as dying, and, behold, we live; as chastened, and not killed; [10]As sorrowful, yet alway rejoicing; as poor, yet making many rich; as having nothing, and yet possessing all things." What an example of suffering for the good of the Kingdom!! Although there is no suffering you, Paul, Stephen nor I can suffer that will even come close to the sacrificial suffering of Jesus Christ. How would I think I could ever look like Him if I never undergo any tribulations?

The 6th reason for pain and suffering in the life of the believer is to develop intimacy with Christ. Indeed, I believe this to be the greatest and the most important of all. If, indeed you come to an understanding of this deep intimacy with Christ Jesus, it changes forever how you view pain and suffering. It did for Paul as he wrote, Phillippians 3: [3]"For we are the circumcision, which worship God in the spirit, and rejoice in Christ Jesus, and have no confidence in the flesh. [4]Though I might also have confidence in the flesh. If any other man thinketh that he hath whereof he might trust in the flesh, I more: [5]Circumcised the eighth day, of the stock of Israel, of the tribe of Benjamin, an Hebrew of the Hebrews; as touching the law, a Pharisee; [6]Concerning zeal, persecuting the church; touching the righteousness which is in the law, blameless. [7]But what things were gain to me, those I counted loss for Christ. [8]Yea doubtless, and I count all things but loss for the excellency of the knowledge of Christ Jesus my Lord: for whom I have suffered the loss of all things, and do count them but dung, that I may win Christ, [9]And be found in him, not having mine own righteousness, which is of the law, but that which is through the faith of Christ, the righteousness which is of God by faith: [10]That I may know him, and the power of his resurrection, and the fellowship of his sufferings, being made conformable unto his death; [11]If by any means I might attain unto the resurrection of the dead." What more can be said than the savoring of these words. I count all things loss, but for the excellency of the knowledge of Christ Jesus my Lord. Nothing, no one, is as important as coming to know Christ in all His Glory. To see Him in all His Magnificent Splendor and to fall before Him and wash His feet with my tears is worth more than anything that I could own or possess on this earth. There is no pain or sorrow too great to endure just for a glimpse of HIM. He is so worthy of my praise that even if there was nothing on the line, I would praise Him. Even if salvation was not on the table, I would still fall before His throne to praise Him. There is no pain, tear, sorrow that I would not willingly walk through again just for the wonderful chance of knowing Him.

Given these as the reasons for Christian Suffering, perhaps, we can begin to understand James when he wrote, James 1: [2]"My brethren, count it all joy when ye fall into divers temptations; [3]Knowing this, that the trying of your faith worketh patience. [4]But let patience have her perfect work, that ye may be perfect and entire, wanting nothing. [5]If any of you lack wisdom, let him ask of God, that giveth to all men liberally, and upbraideth not; and it shall be given him." Or Peter, in I Peter 5: [6]"Humble yourselves therefore under the mighty hand of God, that he may exalt you in due time: [7]Casting all your care upon him; for he careth for you. [8]Be sober, be vigilant; because your adversary the devil, as a roaring lion, walketh about, seeking whom he may devour: [9]Whom resist stedfast in the faith, knowing that the same afflictions are accomplished in your brethren that are in the world. [10]But the God of all grace, who hath called us unto his eternal glory by Christ Jesus, after that ye have suffered a while, make you perfect, stablish, strengthen, settle you. [11] To him be glory and dominion for ever and ever. Amen" And also as Paul wrote, in Romans 5: . "Therefore being justified by faith, we have peace with God through our Lord Jesus Christ: [2]By whom also we have access by faith into this grace wherein we stand, and rejoice in hope of the glory of God. [3]And not only so, but we glory in tribulations also: knowing that tribulation worketh patience; [4]And patience, experience; and experience, hope: [5]And hope maketh not ashamed; because the love of God is shed abroad in our hearts by the Holy Ghost which is given unto us."

Would I Love You Even More

I felt the searing, pelting rain
Deep within my soul
I was uncertain where to turn
Or what should be my goal
I gazed upon a cross so far
That stood upon a hill
A Lion strong had died a Lamb
He gave His life at will
That I so undeserving be
Might see His face of love
A Glimpse of His true Glory
To fill me with His Love

Would I love You just the same
When my life is filled with shame
When pain is all I know
Would my love for You still show
Can I show Your Glory still
Accept this as Your will
When my heart is broke in two
Cradled in Your hands, renew
As on Your hope I soar
Would I love You even more?

CHAPTER 5

Peter's Failure

Luke 22: ³¹And the Lord said, Simon, Simon, behold, Satan hath desired to have you, that he may sift you as wheat:

³²But I have prayed for thee, that thy faith fail not: and when thou art converted, strengthen thy brethren.

³³And he said unto him, Lord, I am ready to go with thee, both into prison, and to death.

³⁴And he said, I tell thee, Peter, the cock shall not crow this day, before that thou shalt thrice deny that thou knowest me.

⁵⁴Then took they him, and led him, and brought him into the high priest's house. And Peter followed afar off.

⁵⁵And when they had kindled a fire in the midst of the hall, and were set down together, Peter sat down among them.

⁵⁶But a certain maid beheld him as he sat by the fire, and earnestly looked upon him, and said, This man was also with him.

⁵⁷And he denied him, saying, Woman, I know him not.

⁵⁸And after a little while another saw him, and said, Thou art also of them. And Peter said, Man, I am not.

⁵⁹And about the space of one hour after another confidently affirmed, saying, Of a truth this fellow also was with him: for he is a Galilaean.

⁶⁰And Peter said, Man, I know not what thou sayest. And immediately, while he yet spake, the cock crew.
⁶¹And the Lord turned, and looked upon Peter. And Peter remembered the word of the Lord, how he had said unto him, Before the cock crow, thou shalt deny me thrice.
⁶²And Peter went out, and wept bitterly.

*P*eter's spirit at that point was broken—whatever concept of himself he had before this denial was suddenly crushed into the realization that he even being warned could not stand a single night without betraying His Lord and Savior. This the same Peter who had so boldly declared that Christ was the Son of God, the same one who walked on the water, and only a few hours prior declared that he was willing to go to prison or death with Christ. A few hours later here he was having denied his Lord 3 times. Imagine the scene of a rugged fisherman sobbing bitterly from his broken spirit, broken and contrite heart. How could that have happened? Had he not been warned by Christ himself? Couldn't he have done better than that? After all, he had walked side by side with Jesus. His was the same brokenness, same questions, same declarations of "never could I betray you, Lord" as mine before my failures. I have the Holy Spirit and the gospel with me. I have walked with Christ for 50 years. I, like Peter, have no excuses that can be rationalized within my own life and heart. He was devastated by that glimpse of Jesus who in the midst of being beaten and accused took a moment to glimpse over at this His disciple with eyes of compassion and love. Though He had warned Peter, He knew the depth of brokenness this would create in the heart of this His follower. A careful dissection of these text and then later the restoration, I am certain will help you and me when we too fail Christ.

Up to this point in time, Simon Peter has been always eagerly pressing forward for the cause of Christ. Peter had grown to love his Savior so passionately that sometimes Peter would leap forward and even dare to defend Christ when no defense was necessary. He continued as such a passionate follower of Christ full of zeal and energy—desiring to please. Sometimes we too can be passionate for Christ, without the understanding needed for that situation. This was the case with Peter who passionately wanted to protect Christ and did not fully understand the full purpose of Christ's need to die to provide the propitiation for the sin of mankind. This was shown in Matthew 16." : ²¹From that time on Jesus began to explain to his disciples that he must go to Jerusalem and suffer many things at the hands of the elders, chief priests and teachers of the law, and that he must be killed and on the third day be raised to life. ²²Peter took him aside and began to rebuke him. "Never, Lord!" he said. "This shall never happen to you!" ²³Jesus turned and said to Peter, "Get behind me, Satan! You are a stumbling block to me; you do not have in mind the things of God, but the things of men." ²⁴Then Jesus said to his disciples, "If anyone would come after me, he must deny himself and take up his cross and follow me. ²⁵For whoever wants to save his life[h] will lose it, but whoever loses his life for me will find it. ²⁶What good will it be for a man if he gains the whole world, yet forfeits his soul? Or what can a man give in exchange for his soul? ²⁷For the Son of Man is going to come in his Father's glory with his angels, and then he will reward each person according to what he has done. ²⁸I tell you the truth, some who are standing here will not taste death before they see the Son of Man coming in his kingdom" Our zeal for Christ does need to be accompanied by sincere knowledge as to God's plan and/or the patience to allow God to unfold the plan. Zeal is a good thing when tempered by the word of God; yet, zeal can rush ahead with great destruction.

Another problem that was present which would demand sifting before Peter could be fully used of Christ in the ministry; was that of pride. Peter had answered the questions appropriately as to who Christ was. He had walked on the water when Christ called out to him. He wanted to defend Christ. He cut off the ear of the soldier with his sword. He was certain he was prepared and ready to do anything for Christ. He was certain that he loved more than any of the other apostles. So often as Christians we believe that we are able to go out and battle for Christ; forgetting that He must do the work through us. We want to claim a part in our sanctification as though we could do any part of the work ourselves. We look around us and think, we love and serve Christ better than those around us? So quick to compare or criticize. Peter knew that Jesus was Christ the Son of the Living God; yet, just as frequently the case with us—he did not grasp the fullest magnitude of what that truly meant. This is noted when in Luke 22 "²⁴And there was also a strife among them, which of them should be accounted the greatest." This can only occur when one believes somewhere inside there is something innately worthy to have rank with Jesus. To be the servant of ministry that Peter was being molded for, he had to learn to trust only in Christ's righteousness and strength—not his own.

So with that background we come to the present scripture. Christ began by telling Simon (using his earthly name) that Satan had requested to sift him like wheat. It is of extreme importance here to note that Satan had to request permission before he could tempt Simon Peter. Unless God said yes, Satan could not have shaken up the faith of Simon Peter to this extent testing its sincerity. Every detail of my life, every temptation, has been ordained by my heavenly Father either by His direct or permissive will. Only He knows what it will take to change this wayward heart of mine. Not only does He allow Satan to test us, He already knows our response. He already knew what Peter's response was going to be and I daresay, He already had the plan for Peter's restoration. With God there is no "OOPS, I didn't see that one coming; now what are we going to do?" So, sometimes He allows Satan to sift us; however, this omnipotent, omniscient, sovereign Creator of the Universe knows exactly what is needed to transform a heart into His image.

Christ told Peter that He had prayed for him that his faith might be sustained and that once he had turned to strengthen his brethren. Imagine that. Christ is interceding for us that God Himself will sustain our faith as we go through fiery trials and temptations. What greater advocate could anyone have? Beyond that Christ said "when thou art converted". It was not a question of if Peter would "make it through"; that was certain because it depended on a Sovereign God who still reigns on His throne. He knew that Peter would deny Him; yet, He knew that this would also become the stepping stone toward a radical transformation of Peter. Peter needed to take his eyes off himself and focus on Christ. He needed to rely upon a faith and righteousness that came from God and not one which Peter could "tighten the belt, try harder, and do better."

Christ did not step in to prevent Satan from sifting Simon Peter. He did not step in and change Peter's outcome. He did; turn to look upon Peter's face once the denial was complete. He wasn't disappointed in Peter, He knew what was going to happen even before it did. So there is no room for disappointment here. But He looked over at Peter, I believe with eyes of compassion and empathy because He knew the anguish that had suddenly filled Peter's heart for this betrayal. He could feel the breaking of Peter's heart and knew the broken spirit that would follow shortly. He felt Peter's pain over Peter's denial. That is what this compassionate Shepherd was concerned about. He knew that the pain was necessary to help Peter to grow; yet, He knew there was great pain and sorrow that morning for a weary, confused, and fatigued disciple. Still, He knew that in order to ever be able to provide communion between Peter and Himself, He still had to walk forward and bare the Cross. He still had to die as the spotless lamb and be raised again to the Father's right hand as the Lion, King of Judah. It is then He became ultimately worthy of Glory. He took my place and Peter's place and your place on that cross so that never again would we be separated from His presence.

But what about Peter, now crushed beneath his own sense of guilt? We know that God had a plan to save Peter; but did He have a plan to use Him in ministry? For each of His children, God has a plan of restoration for each time we fail Him. If I believe that God always has the plan of restoration, would that liberalize me to not care and to just press on with sin as a major part of my life? Just like Paul kept reminding us in Romans, 1000 times no. If I truly know Christ in all His Glory how could I ever willingly cause Him even a second of pain, compassion and sorrow while He watches me stumble into my own failure. Once upon a time, I asked God, "Why God have you broken my heart again?" It was there, that moment that I realized He had not broken my heart; but rather, I had broke His heart. He stood there with all I ever needed and I kept searching for something more. If you have been recently sifted by Satan, know this, if you know Christ as your Savior-He has already prayed and secured the sustainment of your faith through it. He also has a plan for your restoration just as He did Peter.

When I First Came to Know Him

When I first came to know him
So many years ago
I vowed that I would serve him
With heart and mind and soul
Then I found that in my strength
I would but only fail
Then He came and He told me
As we walked down life's trail

1st chorus
I'll be your strength when you are weary
And your hope when skies are gray
I'll be your faith when yours is failing
And your light on each dark day
I'll be the love your lonely heart
When it's breaking in despair
I'll be all in all your everything
If you look to me in prayer

I strove on in my strength
And strayed so very far
Until my life was broken
And sin had left it's scar

Then I cried, Oh, my Father
How deeply I had failed
Then He came and He held me
And His love prevailed

2nd Chorus
Now He's my strength when I am weary
And my hope when skies are gray
He is my faith when mine is failing
And my light on each dark day
He is the love to my lonely heart
When it's breaking in despair
He is all in all my everything
When I look to him in prayer

Now if you have strayed from
Or never knew His love
Then turn your eyes toward Jesus
And seek Him from above
He will take all your brokenness
And fill it with Himself
He will take all your sin away
And fill each empty shelf.

3rd Chorus
He'll be your strength when you are weary
And your hope when skies are gray
He'll be your faith when yours is failing
And your light on each dark day
He'll be the love to your lonely heart
When it's breaking in despair
He'll be all in all your everything
If you look to Him in prayer

CHAPTER 6

Peter's Restoration

John 21: ³Simon Peter saith unto them, I go a fishing. They say unto him, We also go with thee. They went forth, and entered into a ship immediately; and that night they caught nothing.

⁴But when the morning was now come, Jesus stood on the shore: but the disciples knew not that it was Jesus.

⁵Then Jesus saith unto them, Children, have ye any meat? They answered him, No.

⁶And he said unto them, Cast the net on the right side of the ship, and ye shall find. They cast therefore, and now they were not able to draw it for the multitude of fishes.

⁷Therefore that disciple whom Jesus loved saith unto Peter, It is the Lord. Now when Simon Peter heard that it was the Lord, he girt his fisher's coat unto him, (for he was naked,) and did cast himself into the sea.

⁸And the other disciples came in a little ship; (for they were not far from land, but as it were two hundred cubits,) dragging the net with fishes.

⁹As soon then as they were come to land, they saw a fire of coals there, and fish laid thereon, and bread.

¹⁰Jesus saith unto them, Bring of the fish which ye have now caught.

¹¹Simon Peter went up, and drew the net to land full of great fishes, an

hundred and fifty and three: and for all there were so many, yet was not the net broken.

¹²Jesus saith unto them, Come and dine. And none of the disciples durst ask him, Who art thou? knowing that it was the Lord.

¹³Jesus then cometh, and taketh bread, and giveth them, and fish likewise.

¹⁴This is now the third time that Jesus shewed himself to his disciples, after that he was risen from the dead.

¹⁵So when they had dined, Jesus saith to Simon Peter, Simon, son of Jonas, lovest thou me more than these? He saith unto him, Yea, Lord; thou knowest that I love thee. He saith unto him, Feed my lambs.

¹⁶He saith to him again the second time, Simon, son of Jonas, lovest thou me? He saith unto him, Yea, Lord; thou knowest that I love thee. He saith unto him, Feed my sheep.

¹⁷He saith unto him the third time, Simon, son of Jonas, lovest thou me? Peter was grieved because he said unto him the third time, Lovest thou me? And he said unto him, Lord, thou knowest all things; thou knowest that I love thee. Jesus saith unto him, Feed my sheep.

The scene for Peter's restoration takes him back to the very beginning when Christ asked him to follow and He would make him "fisher of men" Christ had reappeared to Simon Peter at two times before this visit; but the time was not right yet until now to ease this apostle's pain. No mention had been made of the denial. This was His third visit as though the number 3 would play a role in this restoration. Jesus Christ in His Omniscience is very patient to wait until the perfect moment. He could have rushed to Simon Peter with the words "I forgive you"; but he didn't. He waited. He knew that Peter was hurting and most likely tried to avoid the obvious question; yet, Jesus waited. It reminds me of another time when Jesus waited despite the pain of another loved one, because he loved them. That time was in John 11 which details Lazarus's death and resurrection. The scriptures read, "¹Now a certain man was sick, named Lazarus, of Bethany, the town of Mary and her sister Martha.

²(It was that Mary which anointed the Lord with ointment, and wiped his feet with her hair, whose brother Lazarus was sick.) ³Therefore his sisters sent unto him, saying, Lord, behold, he whom thou lovest is sick. ⁴When Jesus heard that, he said, This sickness is not unto death, but for the glory of God, that the Son of God might be glorified thereby. ⁵Now Jesus loved Martha, and her sister, and Lazarus. ⁶When he had heard therefore that he was sick, he abode two days still in the same place where he was." In this case it was because He loved Mary, Martha, and Lazarus—He waited so that His Glory might be accomplished and so that they would come to understand His might and power in their life. Had He arrived sooner they could not understand what He was doing. They would have been seeking merely the miracle; but not the miracle giver. They needed to have their faith stretched to the point of faithless sorrow so that they might understand the depth, breadth, and width of His Love and Gift for them. The same is true of Simon Peter, because Christ loved him so much, he had to wait until the perfect moment. Peter had seen the resurrection of Christ and was thrilled with the truth of Christ's death and resurrection; yet, as you note—He returned to fishing. "After all, Christ has said nothing about the denial; perhaps, I cannot be used in His service", thought Peter. "I blew it!! What can I do? I witnessed a miracle beyond any miracle and I met the Savior, the Messiah. What an honor I have been blessed with." So with that mentality, Peter went back to the fishing. That was the only occupation he knew and certainly he did not believe he would ever be good enough to return to Christ's service. He had failed Christ at a crucial moment, all his bragging about love and devotion had been nothing more than a lot of worthless hot air.

Peter had fished all night and even then failed to catch any fish; perhaps, even in this he felt a failure. As the morning dawned there was Christ standing on the shore. In fact, the disciples did not recognize Him; perhaps, they weren't looking for Him at that moment—they were not certain what role they now played in the Kingdom of God. In fact, for Peter, he had gone back to his former life, why would Christ appear now? Peter, I daresay, doesn't recall the prayer and promise of Christ that when he was restored to strengthen the brethren. Instead, Peter took them fishing. In fact, Peter was fishing in the nude as he had formerly done. Then Peter realized that this was Jesus Christ as He had commanded them to throw the nets in and pull up an overflowing catch of fish; just like in the beginning. Peter grabbed his coat and jumped into the water. Oddly, that he would throw on a coat to swim when swimming is much simpler in the nude. Yet, Peter wanted to try to cover his own shame for his lack of faith in Christ's ability to use him and for his denial a few days, weeks prior. When Peter and the disciples reached the shore Christ was already cooking fish so as to provide a meal to His disciples. He attended first to their physical need of hunger before stepping into the important work of restoration. That would be just like Jesus; he would attend to the physical needs so that there would be abundant energy to go about the task at hand. Sometimes in the Christian walk when we awaken in that same position as Peter in which we feel we have failed so severely that we could not be used ever again. At that moment, many times God sends forth just the right song or sermon or person to fill our hungry heart before He begins that work of restoration. Once his hunger had been met, Christ invited Peter for a private walk along the beach. We know this walk is private because while they are talking, it is noted in verse 20 "Then Peter, turning about, seeth the disciple whom Jesus loved following" They had to be walking a few steps ahead and speaking softly.

So they begin this walk, Peter hardly able to contain himself with the thoughts most likely running through his mind. It was the first time they were alone and Christ wanted to talk to him. Then came the piercing questions in a series of three; just like the denial had been a series of three so too the restoring questions are a series of three. Peter prior to the incident was so confident that he loved Christ better than the other disciples and that he would go to prison or death because of his love for Christ. Yet, Peter, came to realize that his own love was not perfect; instead he needed to rest on the assurance that Christ's love was all sufficient. So it is that Christ asked Peter "Simon, son of Jonah, lovest thou me?" Note that Christ once more is calling Peter by his human name and not the spiritual name he had been given. Another point of great interest is the word "lovest", In the latin languages, there are various distinctly different words that refer to love. One type of love is "agape" love. This is an unconditional, never failing, God like love. The other word for love that is used in these verses is phileo love (this refers to a general brother-like love) and would be considered a good type of love; but certainly, with limitations and flaws. It is more like an affection rather than a steady burning, unconditional love. Therefore, the conversation went something like this. Christ said, "Simon, do you love me with a burning, unconditional agape love?" Peter's response is "yeah Lord, I love you with an affectionate, brother like Phileo love." Christ commands Peter to feed his sheep. Remember once more this is the same Peter who had previously swore his love to be greater than anyone's and now he hesitates in his own description of his love for Christ, doubting the depth and sincerity of it. . So, Christ again asks Peter, "Simon, do you love me with a burning, unconditional agape love?" Peter's response again is "yeah Lord, I love you with an affectionate, brother like Phileo love" Christ commands Peter once more to feed his sheep, as demonstration of that love and devotion—He is calling Peter into service again. Then on the third question, Christ asks; "Simon, do you love with an affectionate, brother like love?" What a grievous question. Peter must have quickly thought as I have at times thought, "Lord is my ability to love you so flawed that I cannot even attempt to demonstrate it, does it not even show?" Yet, very humbly, Peter now replies: "Lord, you know all things, look into my heart Lord and You will not need to ask such a question." Once more the Lord calls Peter into service with "Feed my sheep"

Peter had come to realize that he, himself was nothing and had nothing to boast of except for Jesus Christ. He came to realize that in the power of his own love, he would fail. His self-righteous spirit was broken completely. His heart had been broken for Christ and now restored was a humble heart that recognized that unless it is Christ's love and work through him, there was no work at all. Now with all self pride stripped away, Peter was ready to become the preacher he needed to be. He found his own central core of hope in future grace set firm in Jesus Christ and Christ Alone-"the hope for Glory" As Peter writes in I Peter 1: "Who by him do believe in God, that raised him up from the dead, and gave him **glory**; that your faith and **hope** might be in God." No longer could Peter's hope and faith be in himself or even his ability to love Christ; rather, he depended and rested upon the love of God to sustain him and to work out this faith through him. That is why Peter was able to preach at Pentecost where 3000 were saved. It was no longer Peter's boisterous voice; but Christ's voice through Peter. God did not cause Peter to fail; but God did allow Satan to sift Peter and God took Peter's failure and used it for Peter's growth, the increased intimacy with Christ for Peter, and for the good of the kingdom. What an amazing God of Grace and Mercy and Love. God knew that the only source of joy, hope, strength and peace for Peter was an intimate relationship with God. Prior to Peter falling deeply with a broken spirit, broken heart and contrite heart; Peter's pride stood in the way of this intimacy. Peter sometimes had trouble hearing the truth as he was caught up in his own desires. This was not the case with the restored Peter.

It was Peter's own experience that lead him to write in I Peter 1: "³Blessed be the God and Father of our Lord Jesus Christ, which according to his abundant mercy hath begotten us again unto a lively hope by the resurrection of Jesus Christ from the dead,

⁴To an inheritance incorruptible, and undefiled, and that fadeth not away, reserved in heaven for you,
⁵Who are kept by the power of God through faith unto salvation ready to be revealed in the last time.
⁶Wherein ye greatly rejoice, though now for a season, if need be, ye are in heaviness through manifold temptations:
⁷That the trial of your faith, being much more precious than of gold

that perisheth, though it be tried with fire, might be found unto praise and honour and glory at the appearing of Jesus Christ:"

Was Satan about the business of sifting you lately? I daresay that he seems to be consistently having to sift something else from this wayward heart. For a moment, it is very painful; yet, I am much quicker now to turn to Christ and ask "What do I need to learn, Lord? Please show me what you have for me to do? Strengthen me, sustain me and transform me into Your image—whatever it takes". God honors that kind of sincere prayer brought out of a broken spirit, a broken and contrite heart.

FEAR WALKED IN

Fear walked in
I let her stay
And Talk with me a while
What harm was she
A lonely soul
She could not mean me guile

But as she talked
With gentle voice
I listened to her tale
It seemed to touch
A chord in me
My heart began to wale

Jealousy
She was her friend
Who also came to stay
A little while
What could it harm?
As hours turned to days

Another friend
Came close behind
And anger was her name
I could not hear
The voice of God
While playing their wild games

I bid them leave
Get out of here
I screamed at them to go
I let them in
My fault I know
Oh, such a wretched foe

I cried to God
To make them leave
I want to feel your love
I need your joy
Your grandest peace
My eyes to see above

He heard my plea
He bade them leave
My faith He did restore
I felt His love
His warm embrace
How could I want for more?

I looked around
And then I saw
A precious love was gone
I'd lost him there
Oh, wretched self
I knew I'd done such wrong

So if you see
That one called fear
Come knocking at your door
Don't let her in
Bolt tight the locks
Or run to distant shores

Hold tight to God
His truth, His love
And never doubt His word
For fear will bring
Along her friends
Your loss, your fault, Absurd

CHAPTER 7

DAVID-King, Sinner, Broken Spirit and Heart – God's Mercy

Psalm 51

¹Have mercy upon me, O God, according to thy lovingkindness: according unto the multitude of thy tender mercies blot out my transgressions.

²Wash me throughly from mine iniquity, and cleanse me from my sin.

³For I acknowledge my transgressions: and my sin is ever before me.

⁴Against thee, thee only, have I sinned, and done this evil in thy sight: that thou mightest be justified when thou speakest, and be clear when thou judgest.

⁵Behold, I was shapen in iniquity; and in sin did my mother conceive me.

⁶Behold, thou desirest truth in the inward parts: and in the hidden part thou shalt make me to know wisdom.

⁷Purge me with hyssop, and I shall be clean: wash me, and I shall be whiter than snow.

⁸Make me to hear joy and gladness; that the bones which thou hast broken may rejoice.

⁹Hide thy face from my sins, and blot out all mine iniquities.

¹⁰Create in me a clean heart, O God; and renew a right spirit within me.

¹¹Cast me not away from thy presence; and take not thy holy spirit from me.

¹²Restore unto me the joy of thy salvation; and uphold me with thy free spirit.

¹³Then will I teach transgressors thy ways; and sinners shall be converted unto thee.

¹⁴Deliver me from bloodguiltiness, O God, thou God of my salvation: and my tongue shall sing aloud of thy righteousness.

¹⁵O Lord, open thou my lips; and my mouth shall shew forth thy praise.

¹⁶For thou desirest not sacrifice; else would I give it: thou delightest not in burnt offering.

¹⁷The sacrifices of God are a broken spirit: a broken and a contrite heart, O God, thou wilt not despise.

¹⁸Do good in thy good pleasure unto Zion: build thou the walls of Jerusalem.

¹⁹Then shalt thou be pleased with the sacrifices of righteousness, with burnt offering and whole burnt offering: then shall they offer bullocks upon thine altar.

This is the outpouring cry of King David who once recognizing the depth of his own sin against God; fell in utter brokenness of spirit and heart before God. This prayer is one, I have turned to and poured out at the feet of Christ on previous occasions; perhaps, more often than I would wish to remember. But how does this happen to those of us who are called by God to be His servant? What is God's response to this outpouring of true repentance? What about the consequences resulting from the sin? Where do we go from that point? Can we still be used? These are some of the questions I hope to answer with this chapter.

David was a simple shepherd boy that God chose to be a King of Israel. Many years passed between the moment he was chosen and the day he would take the throne. During these years, David grew in his knowledge of God. Part of which must have been learned while tending the sheep on a hillside where he could quietly commune with God in his solitude. After being chosen, he was sent to King Saul's Courtyard as the harpist and musician to soothe the King's evil spirits. Later during a moment of war, David had been sent back to tend the sheep. His father sent him to take food and drink to the frontlines where a Giant Philistine had the army of God paralyzed with fear. David very boldly went forward to request to battle this giant. This famous conversation went like this. I Samuel 17: " 32And David said to Saul, Let no man's heart fail because of him; thy servant will go and fight with this Philistine. 33And Saul said to David, Thou art not able to go against this Philistine to fight with him: for thou art but a youth, and he a man of war from his youth. 34And David said unto Saul, Thy servant kept his father's sheep, and there came a lion, and a bear, and took a lamb out of the flock: 35And I went out after him, and smote him, and delivered it out of his mouth: and when he arose against me, I caught him by his beard, and smote him, and slew him. 36Thy servant slew both the lion and the bear: and this uncircumcised Philistine shall be as one of them, seeing he hath defied the armies of the living God. 37David said moreover, The LORD that delivered me out of the paw of the lion, and out of the paw of the bear, he will deliver me out of the hand of this Philistine. And Saul said unto David, Go, and the LORD be with thee" Armed with a sling, pebbles and God's Mighty Hand; David defeated Goliath. He was brought back to the King's court where he became dear friends with the King's son Jonathan. David continued to fight for the King; but David became very popular with the people and Saul became very jealous. Ultimately David had to run for his life into the hills and caves as Saul looked to kill him.

On two separate occasions, David had the opportunity present in which he could have killed Saul thus opening the door for himself to leave his exile and to take the promised throne. Some would have said, after all God delivered Saul into my hands, why not? Not David, he was truly a noble, honorable man who awaited God's response before acting. In fact, his response was always to let Saul know how close he was while letting Saul escape as is outlined in the following regarding one of the incidences.

I Samuel 24: (NIV) [8] Then David went out of the cave and called out to Saul, "My lord the king!" When Saul looked behind him, David bowed down and prostrated himself with his face to the ground. [9] He said to Saul, "Why do you listen when men say, 'David is bent on harming you'? [10] This day you have seen with your own eyes how the LORD delivered you into my hands in the cave. Some urged me to kill you, but I spared you; I said, 'I will not lift my hand against my master, because he is the LORD's anointed.' [11] See, my father, look at this piece of your robe in my hand! I cut off the corner of your robe but did not kill you. Now understand and recognize that I am not guilty of wrongdoing or rebellion. I have not wronged you, but you are hunting me down to take my life. [12] May the LORD judge between you and me. And may the LORD avenge the wrongs you have done to me, but my hand will not touch you. [13] As the old saying goes, 'From evildoers come evil deeds,' so my hand will not touch you."
[16] When David finished saying this, Saul asked, "Is that your voice, David my son?" And he wept aloud. [17] "You are more righteous than I," he said. "You have treated me well, but I have treated you badly. [18] You have just now told me of the good you did to me; the LORD delivered me into your hands, but you did not kill me. [19] When a man finds his enemy, does he let him get away unharmed? May the LORD reward you well for the way you treated me today. [20] I know that you will surely be king and that the kingdom of Israel will be established in your hands. [21] Now swear to me by the LORD that you will not cut off my descendants or wipe out my name from my father's family."

²² So David gave his oath to Saul. Then Saul returned home, but David and his men went up to the stronghold.

And then on the second occasion, David had the opportunity to kill Saul, he again refused to harm Saul who had continued to seek to kill him.

I Samuel 26 (NIV) ⁷ So David and Abishai went to the army by night, and there was Saul, lying asleep inside the camp with his spear stuck in the ground near his head. Abner and the soldiers were lying around him.

⁸ Abishai said to David, "Today God has delivered your enemy into your hands. Now let me pin him to the ground with one thrust of my spear; I won't strike him twice."

⁹ But David said to Abishai, "Don't destroy him! Who can lay a hand on the LORD's anointed and be guiltless? ¹⁰ As surely as the LORD lives," he said, "the LORD himself will strike him; either his time will come and he will die, or he will go into battle and perish. ¹¹ But the LORD forbid that I should lay a hand on the LORD's anointed. Now get the spear and water jug that are near his head, and let's go."

¹² So David took the spear and water jug near Saul's head, and they left. No one saw or knew about it, nor did anyone wake up. They were all sleeping, because the LORD had put them into a deep sleep.

¹³ Then David crossed over to the other side and stood on top of the hill some distance away; there was a wide space between them. ¹⁴ He called out to the army and to Abner son of Ner, "Aren't you going to answer me, Abner?"

Abner replied, "Who are you who calls to the king?"

¹⁵ David said, "You're a man, aren't you? And who is like you in Israel? Why didn't you guard your lord the king? Someone came to destroy your lord the king. ¹⁶ What you have done is not good. As surely as the LORD lives, you and your men deserve to die, because you did not guard your master, the LORD's anointed. Look around you. Where are the king's spear and water jug that were near his head?"

17 Saul recognized David's voice and said, "Is that your voice, David my son?"

David replied, "Yes it is, my lord the king." 18 And he added, "Why is my lord pursuing his servant? What have I done, and what wrong am I guilty of? 19 Now let my lord the king listen to his servant's words. If the LORD has incited you against me, then may he accept an offering. If, however, men have done it, may they be cursed before the LORD! They have now driven me from my share in the LORD's inheritance and have said, 'Go, serve other gods.' 20 Now do not let my blood fall to the ground far from the presence of the LORD. The king of Israel has come out to look for a flea—as one hunts a partridge in the mountains."

21 Then Saul said, "I have sinned. Come back, David my son. Because you considered my life precious today, I will not try to harm you again. Surely I have acted like a fool and have erred greatly."

22 "Here is the king's spear," David answered. "Let one of your young men come over and get it. 23 The LORD rewards every man for his righteousness and faithfulness. The LORD delivered you into my hands today, but I would not lay a hand on the LORD's anointed. 24 As surely as I valued your life today, so may the LORD value my life and deliver me from all trouble."

25 Then Saul said to David, "May you be blessed, my son David; you will do great things and surely triumph."

So David went on his way, and Saul returned home.

After this, David left the country until he heard that Saul had died. Following this, David was placed on the throne. God made a covenant with David. Included in this covenant, 2 Samuel 7 says,, "13He shall build an house for my name, and I will stablish the throne of his kingdom for ever. 14I will be his father, and he shall be my son. **If he commit iniquity, I will chasten him with the rod of men, and with the stripes of the children of men: 15But my mercy shall not depart away from him**, as I took it from Saul, whom I put away before thee. "Note the very significance of these words. On multiple occasions, there is noted that "the spirit of the Lord had left Saul" This we may see as strange and believe that somehow it indicates our ability to be "lost" after salvation, but it doesn't. In fact, it proves that whoever comes in true faith has eternal security established by God's own power to keep and not our own. Many times our question might be why David and not Saul? Why does God choose one and not another? Everyone that is born at some time reaches a point of God where a choice is made as to yes or no. God stands and knocks at each door or each heart; yet, He already knows who will and will not accept Him. Sometimes He continues to knock for many years, sometimes He only knocks once, so there is no room for "later" when responding. Some people would try to say that God is unjust not to just save everyone; but the truth is we are all so unworthy that it is truly amazing that He would choose anyone and particularly me. He sees something in the heart of faith and devotion to Himself that He exchanges for His righteousness as the gift of salvation. The truth is as He foreshadowed His position with David through this His covenant and promise. If he commit adultery, I will chasten him; but mercy will not depart from Him." God knew that David would fail because God is omniscient. This was not a promise which God made and later regretted having done so. God knew about Bathsheba and Urriah even before it happened and despite that, He made this covenant with David. That is true of each and every one that has ever accepted Christ as their Savior. He knows every sin and every thought you or I will ever have, and He saves us just the same. What wondrous Grace and Mercy is that!!

David kept his promise and brought one of Saul's sons to his court, establishing the return of their land to Saul's heirs. He was a very successful and wise King, until one day or one season, he sinned. This is recorded in 2 Samuel 11: "¹And it came to pass, after the year was expired, at the time when kings go forth to battle, that David sent Joab, and his servants with him, and all Israel; and they destroyed the children of Ammon, and besieged Rabbah. But David tarried still at Jerusalem.

²And it came to pass in an eveningtide, that David arose from off his bed, and walked upon the roof of the king's house: and from the roof he saw a woman washing herself; and the woman was very beautiful to look upon.

³And David sent and enquired after the woman. And one said, Is not this Bathsheba, the daughter of Eliam, the wife of Uriah the Hittite?

⁴And David sent messengers, and took her; and she came in unto him, and he lay with her; for she was purified from her uncleanness: and she returned unto her house.

⁵And the woman conceived, and sent and told David, and said, I am with child." As you note this was the time that the kings go forth and he had stayed at home. Perhaps he had grown content and complacent; and just a little proud. Whatever his reason, David was not where he was suppose to be. How frequently is that the case with me and you? We just are not where we are suppose to be and that makes us vulnerable to whatever temptation arises. But after the one night affair, certainly, David probably thought. Oh well, no real harm done. It is past anyway, no one will have to know the truth. No one hurt, God won't care too much. Of course, I am imagining what he thought by putting in the same excuses I or you have used in the past after such an indiscretion. Yet, Bathesheba became pregnant and now there was a problem. Her husband was out at war. David called for him to try to cover up by trying to get him to go home and sleep with his wife, Bathsheba. However, Urriah was by far more noble than David at that time and would not see his wife because as recorded in 2 Samuel 11, "And Uriah said unto David, The ark, and Israel, and Judah, abide in tents; and my lord Joab, and the servants of my lord, are encamped in the open fields; shall I then go into mine house, to eat and to drink, and to lie with my wife? as thou livest, and as thy soul liveth, I will not do this thing" This was one of David's finest and noblest of soldiers and for that reason, David sent orders to send him to the forefront and then withdraw so that he might die in battle. What a sordid plan of a powerful King. He only wanted to clean up this mess he made while preserving his own reputation. What

happened to the noble man who had listened so closely to God? It so happens that when we find ourselves where we are not suppose to be, we probably quit listening as intently as we had been.

With Urriah dead, David could bring the widow of this "fallen Hero" for Israel to his court and look like such a great guy as long as no one really finds out. The thing is God knew and no amount of cover-up to remove the facts of what had happened. Nathan then came to David and told him this story. 2 Samuel 12: " ¹And the LORD sent Nathan unto David. And he came unto him, and said unto him, There were two men in one city; the one rich, and the other poor.

²The rich man had exceeding many flocks and herds:
³But the poor man had nothing, save one little ewe lamb, which he had bought and nourished up: and it grew up together with him, and with his children; it did eat of his own meat, and drank of his own cup, and lay in his bosom, and was unto him as a daughter.
⁴And there came a traveller unto the rich man, and he spared to take of his own flock and of his own herd, to dress for the wayfaring man that was come unto him; but took the poor man's lamb, and dressed it for the man that was come to him.
⁵And David's anger was greatly kindled against the man; and he said to Nathan, As the LORD liveth, the man that hath done this thing shall surely die:
⁶And he shall restore the lamb fourfold, because he did this thing, and because he had no pity.
⁷And Nathan said to David, Thou art the man. Thus saith the LORD God of Israel, I anointed thee king over Israel, and I delivered thee out of the hand of Saul;
⁸And I gave thee thy master's house, and thy master's wives into thy bosom, and gave thee the house of Israel and of Judah; and if that had been too little, I would moreover have given unto thee such and such things.

⁹"Wherefore hast thou despised the commandment of the LORD, to do evil in his sight? thou hast killed Uriah the Hittite with the sword, and hast taken his wife to be thy wife, and hast slain him with the sword of the children of Ammon.

¹⁰Now therefore the sword shall never depart from thine house; because thou hast despised me, and hast taken the wife of Uriah the Hittite to be thy wife.

¹¹Thus saith the LORD, Behold, I will raise up evil against thee out of thine own house, and I will take thy wives before thine eyes, and give them unto thy neighbour, and he shall lie with thy wives in the sight of this sun.

¹²For thou didst it secretly: but I will do this thing before all Israel, and before the sun.

¹³And David said unto Nathan, I have sinned against the LORD. And Nathan said unto David, The LORD also hath put away thy sin; thou shalt not die.

¹⁴Howbeit, because by this deed thou hast given great occasion to the enemies of the LORD to blaspheme, the child also that is born unto thee shall surely die." That is when David with his eyes wide open regarding his sin went to God in prayer with that which is recorded in Psalm 51.

David realized that in the final analysis of things all sin is against God and God alone. He recognized the abomination of his own sin and pleaded for God to restore His peace and His joy of the salvation to David. He also came to realize that the most precious thing in God's eyes was man's spirit and heart which had been broken in sorrow for the Glory of God. A heart that no longer sought after its own glory; but rather, followed after whatever would bring more Glory to this wondrous friend and Savior. God honors a contrite heart, humbled by its own failures and standing in awe of a magnificent King of all Kings. This was the repentant David who fell before God's throne stripped of all pride or excuses.

Yes, the baby did die and David's house was filled with many sorrows that followed as remnants and reminders of the consequences of sin. Still, God was with David and guided his steps. He had restored David's peace and joy. And as the greatest gift of mercy and grace, Jesus Christ was born in the direct lineage of David and Bathsheba through Solomon. Despite the sin, the sorrows, the consequences it is noted in I Kings 11: "4For it came to pass, when Solomon was old, that his wives turned away his heart after other gods: and his heart was not perfect with the LORD his God, as was the heart of David his father." Note God referred to David's heart as perfect with the Lord his God. Wow that I might one day stand before God and it be said that My heart was perfect with the Lord My God. That is my greatest desire, is it yours? So the answer to the final question can we still be used after we fail. Yes, a thousand times yes, for David was the line of our dear Savior.

Love Divine
by
Effie Darlene Barba

He comes to me when night is still
I hear his gentle, loving voice
He whispers words or sometimes songs
To help me choose which choice

I feel the warmth of His embrace
When darkness, sorrow fills the air
I feel such comfort, safety there
So far from Satan's lair

So many years I searched to find
A human love, true friend for me
Yet, were there one, oh could I hear
His voice, such clarity

If I were left to choose which path
Is better, higher here to trod
And knew this much as now I know
I surely would choose God

You see, what I had thought was loss
Through tears and pain I now can see
He had a plan, a perfect plan
Of love and joy for me

Though sorrow, pain may be the way
He draws me close and holds me near
I know that He has felt each pain
And cried with me each tear

And though at times I was untrue
His love, His strength His hope is mine
What wondrous joy delight I know
Such gracious love divine

CHAPTER 8

Wherein Lies Your Passion?

Philippians 3: [13]Brethren, I count not myself to have apprehended: but this one thing I do, forgetting those things which are behind, and reaching forth unto those things which are before,
[14]I press toward the mark for the prize of the high calling of God in Christ Jesus.

Throughout this life we develop goals for which we strive to complete. Many times our goals are life stages—finish high school, go to college, find a career, get married, or start a family. For some, it may be to excel in some sport. Some want an Olympic Gold Medal. Whatever goal we seek, our success depends on how passionate are we to complete that goal in life. What are we willing to sacrifice in order to complete that goal? Passion is an intense emotion compelling feeling, enthusiasm, or desire for something. The term is also often applied to a lively or eager interest in or admiration for a proposal, cause, or activity or love. Passion can be expressed as a feeling of unusual excitement, enthusiasm or compelling emotion towards a subject, idea, person, or object. Great athletes generally must rise above the crowd in a passionate pursuit that drives them far beyond the average man. Often they are immune to realizing pain, as they drive themselves past injury, past fatigue in order to finish the race first. They stay focused on the final goal and will sacrifice anything to accomplish that goal. They spend hours and hours in constant hard sacrificial training with the final goal always pressed before them. It is no wonder that Paul used such an analogy to the Christian walk. I am not there yet; but this one most important thing is the only worthy goal for which I place all my passion toward completing. I must forget all the former failures, sorrows, and pains so as to constantly stretch forward to reach that most important of all goals. I press ever forward with training, self denial for the prize of the high calling of God in Christ Jesus. Keeping Christ Jesus as my goal ever before my eyes, I lay aside everything else as unimportant in comparison to knowing Him in all His Glory.

Take a look at the passages just before 13 in Philippians 3: [7]But what things were gain to me, those I counted loss for Christ.

[8]Yea doubtless, and I count all things but loss for the excellency of the knowledge of Christ Jesus my Lord: for whom I have suffered the loss of all things, and do count them but dung, that I may win Christ,
[9]And be found in him, not having mine own righteousness, which is of the law, but that which is through the faith of Christ, the righteousness which is of God by faith:
[10]That I may know him, and the power of his resurrection, and the fellowship of his sufferings, being made conformable unto his death;
[11]If by any means I might attain unto the resurrection of the dead.
[12]Not as though I had already attained, either were already perfect: but I follow after, if that I may apprehend that for which also I am apprehended of Christ Jesus.

So, the question comes within our Christian walk, "Wherein lies your passion?" Is there anything that you see as being so important that everything else pales in comparison? Some would say their spouse or their children are the most important. Some people feel success or position in life is the most important thing. Even at that, often people may think themselves passionate about something only to later find it unimportant—hence divorce, child neglect, and poor work ethics still run rampant in our society. Often in our Christian walk we are rather lackadaisical about our Christian life. We run hot and cold all too often with no true zeal or passion. We lose focus on our goal. Our Bible lays neatly tucked next to our bed and comes out only to accompany us to church on Sunday. Such a precious gift of His Word so that we might come to know Him better by reading and studying it; yet, it frequently lays unopened while we retire to watch TV in the evening or a movie. Could we say, "I count all things loss, for the Excellency of knowing HIM"? After all if TV, Family, the internet, and the phone prevent us from even opening His word would we rather say, "I count Christ loss for the Excellency of knowing and having all this stuff? What are we passionate for? We too often go to prayer and reading the Bible only when there is a crisis in life or when we want things to go a different way. We fall to our knees in prayer and weeping, "Oh, God, please change these circumstances. God where are you? Why did you let me get sick? Why did I lose my job?" But when life is going along ok; did you ever just sit down and talk to Christ Jesus, your best brother and friend? Do you ever look into the sky and just laugh because of the beauty and share that laughter with God? Have you ever gone to work and can't wait to get home to see the next sermon in a series, hands perspiring with the anticipation? Through the day do you hear gospel love songs for God running through your head, as you joyfully go about the tasks of your day? I need to get you awake on this one. Does your heart beat with excitement when you hear a song of worship and praise?

Paul had learned that nothing, absolutely nothing was as important in life as to know Christ Jesus intimately, intensely filling ever crevice of our hearts, minds and souls. He also understood that sometimes we walk through pain or suffering so that we might share in His suffering and grow even deeper IN LOVE with this Blameless Lamb who despite being the powerful Lion of Judah, laid down His Life that we might know Him. What greater love is there than the unconditional, sacrificial love He has for us. His Glory, His Majesty compels our very heart and souls to praise Him. His overwhelming love for me reaches deep inside to transform this heart, so that I might catch a glimpse of what true, pure love is and thus be drawn ever closer to Him. Each year as I see a larger glimpse of Him, I find it so overwhelming that it fills each fiber of my being.

Most of my life I searched for human love, I begged God to give me a companion that could love me. I did marry the love of my life, but he was crippled by bipolar disease and unable to show love. Instead, he was physically and mentally abusive as he cycled through the phases of his illness. Amazingly, God taught me so much about unconditional love and the love of my heavenly Father through all those years. My husband died and I was devastated, he was my whole world (even if at times a sick world of pain and suffering). Yet, before he died he came to know Christ as his Savior and his eternity was changed- God had a perfect plan of love, whether I fully understood it or not. Many of the years of my life I sat alone and felt so desperately filled with loneliness and longing to be loved. During all that time and through bad relationships, I came to realize that never was I alone. God was there in the middle of the night when I cried myself to sleep and God was there the next morning when I would wash my face to go off for work. God was there as I talked to Him about my hopes for the day and to take away my fears while driving to work. He sometimes would awaken me with a song singing in my head at three am so I could smile, go back to sleep and know He already had the answer. I am so grateful that during all those years of loneliness, I was given the awesome opportunity to fall so deeply in love with Jesus that I could never turn back. He became the passion of my heart, as I had been the passion of His when He endured the beatings, the mockery, the pain, His Father's momentary turning of His back, and His death on the Cross just because He loved me.

So, again I must ask you, "Wherein lies Your Passion? Is He, Jesus Christ the most important goal in your life? Are you willing to lose every other dream in order to follow Him? Will you diligently study and train so as to move ever closer to His magnificent Glory? I only hope and pray that you realize that to move ever forward in this Christian walk you need to become passionate about this one thing, as Paul the Apostle was, that everything is unimportant compared to knowing Him and pressing toward the mark for the Prize of the High Calling of our Savior. Ask Him to give you that heart of love for Him and He will. Once there, you will be able to know joy and hope no matter what the circumstances around you; because of the overflowing well of love and life inside you. The more you love God, the more love flows through you and circling back to God and back through you until that becomes an every flowing spiral upward to heaven, overflowing with rivers of living water. Let me share with you this poem and I hope you enjoy it.

A TALK WITH GOD

Oh, let me Lord delight in You
And lay all else I hold aside
For no desire could mean as much
As hear Your voice, to feel your touch
And in Your arms abide

I feel the safety of your arms
Surrounding me throughout each storm
And when the bitter winter wind
Would bid my very spirit bend
Your breath will keep me warm

Forgive me Lord, this fragile heart
Sometimes desires too much
Forgetting You are all I need
Then comes my tears, my plead
To stop and feel Your touch

I then can hear your gentle laugh
The love within Your voice
"My child I love you evermore
My gifts on you I freely pour
The best for you my choice"

Oh, Lord I want to stay right here
And sit here at Your feet
To never step away from You
And then I cannot lose my view
No chance for fear, defeat

"But child I ask then who would go
To tell the wounded broken heart
That I their lonely heart would mend
If not but you, who can I send
If you refuse to start"

Then Father, Dear, I must say yes
To go and run Your bidding do
And You will cast aside my fears
Your hand will wipe away my tears
And keep my eyes on You
I know that You go with me now
You're ever present in my heart
I feel Your joy arise within
I feel Your wondrous strength again
Your love will ne'er depart

CHAPTER 9

God's Armor

Ephesians 6: ¹⁰Finally, my brethren, be strong in the Lord, and in the power of his might.

¹¹Put on the whole armour of God that ye may be able to stand against the wiles of the devil.

¹²For we wrestle not against flesh and blood, but against principalities, against powers, against the rulers of the darkness of this world, against spiritual wickedness in high places.

¹³Wherefore take unto you the whole armour of God, that ye may be able to withstand in the evil day, and having done all, to stand.

¹⁴Stand therefore, having your loins girt about with truth, and having on the breastplate of righteousness;

¹⁵And your feet shod with the preparation of the gospel of peace;

¹⁶Above all, taking the shield of faith, wherewith ye shall be able to quench all the fiery darts of the wicked.

¹⁷And take the helmet of salvation, and the sword of the Spirit, which is the word of God:

¹⁸Praying always with all prayer and supplication in the Spirit, and watching thereunto with all perseverance and supplication for all saints;

*W*hen we think about soldiers going out to battle, we think about the training and preparation and how these are truly brave men and women who would risk their lives for their country. Yet a study of the fact that many are teenagers and many return with post-traumatic stress disorder, indicating that perhaps they were not indeed any different than the rest of us; yet, they were trained to perform. They are groomed and prepped and then sent out where much depends on whether they follow the commander's orders completely. Part of that preparation is in how to properly use their gear and how to protect their own life against the enemy. We are, as Christians constantly engaged in a battle against Satan. At the point of salvation we join God's army. Some would say that is silly, I don't even believe in war—only peace. Ours is a defensive army to ward off attack and destruction. The offensive part of our army is carried forth by God and God alone. It is His wrath against sin which requires payment. He provided a way for sinful man when He poured out His wrath on Christ Jesus who willingly stepped in as substitute. It is God's fury against evil that will be poured out on Satan and all His followers in the final Day of Judgment. In the meantime, all who have been saved by faith in Jesus Christ are a part of God's Army to draw others to a saving knowledge of Christ. Because our work is to bring a dying world to faith in Christ Jesus so they might join the ranks of those who worship and praise the Glorious King of Kings; we are direct targets of Satan who would prefer that all remain blinded to the truth. He wants to destroy every testimony; so, Satan remains very busy about his work. He is the master of disguises and enters in by many forms some of which are religions which confuse and trade away the truth. God has provided us with His armor to protect us through Satan's attacks. Our Father has given us everything that we need to be more than conquerors. If a soldier goes forth to battle without first applying his protective gear, he certainly increases his own risk of defeat. Within Ephesians 6 is outlined for us the armor needed in this battle. He says that with this armor we will be able to stand (not fall, not grapple)—to stand firm, fearless to the very end. So it is important that we recognize the need to put on our armor daily before we are attacked in battle.

We are to stand with our loins girt about with truth. The ancient soldiers had their loins (waist) girt about with a leather belt that held the other pieces of their armor in place. So tightly and firmly about our waist we are to wear the truth which will firmly hold in place the remainder of our armor. So what truth are we talking about? The Bible is rich with the truth of God. There is the truth of the Gospel of Jesus Christ, He who bore our sins and opened the floodgates of communion between God and man for all who will receive Him as their Savior. There is the truth of all the promises of God for provision, strength, joy, hope, peace and sustaining grace. There is the magnificent truth that God the Creator of the Universe with all its innumerable galaxies is still intimately involved in every detail of my little life. It is important that we read and study His word so that we might know the truth especially as Satan knows the scripture so well and knows how to twist it. 2 Timothy 2: "[15]Study to shew thyself approved unto God, a workman that needeth not to be ashamed, rightly dividing the word of truth." We must search prayerfully for God's truth so that our belt holds strong supporting our central framework—keeping us standing strong.

We are also to put on the breastplate of righteousness. We are to be covered with moral conduct that comes from a desire for obedience to the Father. Now by saying this have I returned to "good works of my own volition". No but good works and moral behavior are the byproduct of a heart that is fully seeking after Jesus Christ. Thus the breastplate is to cover the heart of the believer to keep it ever tender to the calls of Christ. The truth of the Scripture helps to hold our breastplate in place. In Hebrews 4 we see:" [12]For the word of God is quick, and powerful, and sharper than any twoedged sword, piercing even to the dividing asunder of soul and spirit, and of the joints and marrow, and is a discerner of the thoughts and intents of the heart." We know from I Samuel 7 that God said "for the LORD seeth not as man seeth; for man looketh on the **outward appearance**, but the LORD looketh on the **heart**." So the question that comes here is, "Is your heart bent toward obeying God?" Do you see Christ in all His glory through the eyes of your Heart so that you are drawn to obey and follow Him? Ephesians 1: [18]"The eyes of your understanding (Heart) being enlightened; that ye may know what is the hope of his calling, and what the riches of the glory of his inheritance in the saints[19]And what is the exceeding greatness of his power to us-ward who believe, according to the working of his mighty power, [20]Which he wrought in Christ, when he raised him from the dead, and set him at his own right hand in the heavenly places" The breastplate is to protect this precious knowledge which draws us to seek to follow after righteousness, desiring it from the central core of your heart.

We are also told to have our "feet shod with the preparation of the gospel of peace." As a soldier we are given here part of the marching orders. Peacefully, we are to spread the gospel. As you may note this did not say mouth, though we are to proclaim the gospel. More importantly we are to live out the gospel through our daily walk and actions. We are to live in such a way as to cause people to be drawn to Christ. By our very actions people are to see the peace, joy, and hope within us. We are to spread the gospel through our kindness and demonstrations of love to a world in need of a Savior. As Christians we are to stand firm in our convictions; but that does not mean we are out picketing and protesting. If we bring sinners to Christ then He will transform their life and behaviors. We are to be ready to go wherever He calls us to and whenever He calls. Unfortunately, too many believe that their testimony is only verbal; yet, their very lifestyle and responses at work and in the public fail to demonstrate Christ. For example, a Church Leader may stand up on Sunday with a beautiful testimony of Christ and then on Monday on the way to work is consumed with road rage and curses another driver. After arriving at work, he may take part in some dishonest business adventure or have an affair or mistreat his employees. In that case has he carried forth the spreading of the gospel?—definitely not. In fact if our walk does not demonstrate Christ we would be better off to keep our mouths shut because we only cause harm to Christ's good news. Our feet should be covered with the gospel first and our mouth follow after we have shown the difference Christ has made in our behavior.

"Above all, taking the shield of faith, wherewith ye shall be able to quench all the fiery darts of the wicked;" we march forth ready to stand firm. I daresay, I have and am continually learning that faith is a crucial part in our being able to win in this battle or at least to make progress. Paul indicated this by his two simple words "Above All". Too often we find that we believe that Christ died to cover our sins and therefore, we have a faith that allows for salvation; but we fail to fully accept that this Sovereign God is going to complete that work of perfecting us so that we look like Christ. We accept that Christ will save us from hell one day; but we tend to doubt that He is in control of every second of our lives. Maybe He is there on Sunday morning while I am sitting in church, but is He there when someone crashes into my car on the way to work Monday morning? He is there when a wonderful bonus check comes in and we rejoice, but do you know that He is there when for no reason your boss fires you? Oddly enough we accept that He loved us enough that He gave His son to die in our place; yet, we can't believe He loves us enough to forgive a lie we told yesterday. We like children run, hide and try to cover up our sin as though this omnipotent, omniscient God didn't already know even before we were saved and He called us to be His anyway. We might believe in His grace of yesterday; but do we believe in His Grace for today and tomorrow? Do we really believe that He is omnipotent and that He has our best interest at heart? If so why do we ever worry about anything? This shield of faith is to divert all of Satans fiery darts. His darts are penetrating and cut deep into our minds if not for our shield of faith. Some of Satan's favorite phrases are "Oh, surely, God didn't say that; after all, God would never deny you that pleasure" "What makes you think God cares about such trivial things?" Another of his favorite phrases is; "How could God ever really love you after you made so many mistakes?" "Use you, look at you, HAHAHA, what could you do for Christ?" "Just wait, God is going to destroy you for what you just did?" "Repent, hogwash, you have plenty of time, just wait until another day when you get older." These darts can wear on us and once we believe them we become open to sin moving in and taking over for a moment or a season. The only strong defense against these darts of doubt is true faith. I don't want to make too lightly of this because faith in God for yesterday, today and tomorrow (future grace is equally present as yesterday's grace) is the central point of our being able to get it right. Our failures in our Christian walk can always be traced back to a failure in faith. Hebrews 11: ¹Now faith is the substance of things hoped for, the evidence of things not seen. ²For by it the elders obtained a good report. ³Through faith we understand that the worlds were framed by the word of God, so that things which are seen were not made of things which do appear. ... ⁶But without faith it is impossible to please him: for he that cometh to God must believe that he is, and that he is a rewarder of them that diligently seek him.

Paul described faith once in Athens by saying as recorded in Acts 17: ²⁴"God that made the world and all things therein, seeing that he is Lord of heaven and earth, dwelleth not in temples made with hands; ²⁵Neither is worshipped with men's hands, as though he needed any thing, seeing he giveth to all life, and breath, and all things; ²⁶And hath made of one blood all nations of men for to dwell on all the face of the earth, and hath determined the times before appointed, and the bounds of their habitation; ²⁷That they should seek the Lord, if haply they might feel after him, and find him, though he be not far from every one of us: ²⁸For in him we live, and move, and have our being; as certain also of your own poets have said, For we are also his offspring. ²⁹Forasmuch then as we are the offspring of God, we ought not to think that the Godhead is like unto gold, or silver, or stone, graven by art and man's device. ³⁰And the times of this ignorance God winked at; but now commandeth all men every where to repent: ³¹Because he hath appointed a day, in the which he will judge the world in righteousness by that man whom he hath ordained; whereof he hath given assurance unto all men, in that he hath raised him from the dead." In this Paul reminds us that to believe means that we see Him as Creator, Sovereign and Savior and that we see everything around us in view of that. As Creator, He owns me. I don't own Him—He created me and my place is to serve Him—not that He serves me. I am not the center focus of my life; everything that I am or have is for His purpose and comes from Him, through Him. As Sovereign He is in complete total control of everything that happens in this world and my life. As Savior He gave His son to die to pay the price of my salvation, and if He did that, He only has good intentions for me. So if He is Creator, Sovereign, and Savior then everything that comes into your life is for your good whether you see that or not. That kind of faith will shred every satanic dart before it even gets close because it perfectly covers you completely.

Also "take the helmet of salvation." Protect your mind from doubts about your salvation. If you ever accepted Christ as your Savior then no one can pluck you out of His hands. Romans 8:"³¹What shall we then say to these things? If God be for us, who can be against us? ³²He that spared not his own Son, but delivered him up for us all, how shall he not with him also freely give us all things? ³³Who shall lay any thing to the charge of God's elect? It is God that justifieth. ³⁴Who is he that condemneth? It is Christ that died, yea rather, that is risen again, who is even at the right hand of God, who also maketh intercession for us. ³⁵Who shall separate us from the love of Christ? Shall tribulation, or distress, or persecution, or famine, or nakedness, or peril, or sword? ³⁶As it is written, For thy sake we are killed all the day long; we are accounted as sheep for the slaughter. ³⁷Nay, in all these things we are more than conquerors through him that loved us. ³⁸For I am persuaded, that neither death, nor life, nor angels, nor principalities, nor powers, nor things present, nor things to come, ³⁹Nor height, nor depth, nor any other creature, shall be able to separate us from the love of God, which is in Christ Jesus our Lord." We keep our mind firm on this assurance of our Salvation. That assurance is based on God Himself; therefore, it is done.

You are armed with two offensive weapons. The first is we are admonished to take with us "the sword of the Spirit, which is the word of God:" This is true from two views of the issue. It is His word that rightly divides the truth. It is His word that has the power to change men's hearts toward Him. To have this sword readily available we need to study the Bible. The Holy Spirit helps us in the understanding of scripture and also helps us to recall whatever scripture we need. John 14: 26 But the **Comforter**, which is the Holy Ghost, whom the Father will send in my name, he shall teach you all things, and bring all things to your remembrance, whatsoever I have said unto you." John 15: 26 tells us that "But when the **Comforter** is come, whom I will send unto you from the Father, even the Spirit of truth, which proceedeth from the Father, he shall testify of me" The entire Bible is a picture of Christ and that too becomes very significant here. The sword is sharp because of Jesus Christ. Look again at John 1: [1]In the beginning was the Word, and the Word was with God, and the Word was God. [2]The same was in the beginning with God. [3]All things were made by him; and without him was not any thing made that was made. [4]In him was life; and the life was the light of men. [5]And the light shineth in darkness; and the darkness comprehended it not. [6]There was a man sent from God, whose name was John. [7]The same came for a witness, to bear witness of the Light, that all men through him might believe. [8]He was not that Light, but was sent to bear witness of that Light. [9]That was the true Light, which lighteth every man that cometh into the world. [10]He was in the world, and the world was made by him, and the world knew him not. [11]He came unto his own, and his own received him not. [12]But as many as received him, to them gave he power to become the sons of God, even to them that believe on his name: [13]Which were born, not of blood, nor of the will of the flesh, nor of the will of man, but of God. [14]And the Word was made flesh, and dwelt among us, (and we beheld his glory, the glory as of the only begotten of the Father,) full of grace and truth. [15]John bare witness of him, and cried, saying, This was he of whom I spake, He that cometh after me is preferred before me: for he was before me. [16]And of his fullness have all we received, and grace for grace.[17]For the law was given by Moses, but grace and truth came by Jesus Christ." The sword of the Spirit is the Word of God which is Jesus Christ, crucified, buried and risen who has forever proclaimed the Victory for the army of the living God. He is the mighty Sword which we are given.

Our other offensive weapon is prayer. "[18]Praying always with all prayer and supplication in the Spirit, and watching thereunto with all perseverance and supplication for all saints;" Jesus Christ separated Himself in prayer with the Father. He taught us that we are to pray to our Heavenly Father to let our requests be made known, to just talk with Him so He can tell us His plans. He whispers His comforting words and He guides each step. Have you talked to Him today. Prayer is one of our greatest privileges that we should jump at the chance. I find myself talking to Him intermittently throughout the day as though a dear friend is shadowing me all day. The truth is He is right there. It is amazing how He shows little glimpses of His mercy throughout the day if you are watching and listening. He warns us at times when danger approaches so that we might be ready.

Amazing He gave us the armor and all we need to do is wear it and stand firm in the days of testing. He is such a mighty Savior, what more could I want.

Little Soldier

Little Soldier are you ready?
The battle cry is here
Little Soldier are you wearing
All your God given gear

Did you put on your helmet?
Remembering what He's done
He provided your salvation
When He gave His only Son

Did you strap on your breastplate?
Is your passion now on Him?
To follow in His footsteps
And shun all willful sin

Did you strap on the waist band?
Holding tight to all God said
And never compromising
So by His truth you are lead

Did you cover yourself completely
By the shield of faith in God
This Sovereign, Omniscient, Shepherd
We are protected by His rod.

So where are we going
To spread the gospel song?
Feet now shod with love and peace
We walk as we belong
So say a prayer, and off we go
To far and distant lands
To spread His gospel to a world
Is all that He demands

CHAPTER 10

The Grace in Which We Stand

Romans 5: ¹Therefore being justified by faith, we have peace with God through our Lord Jesus Christ:
²By whom also we have access by faith into this grace wherein we stand, and rejoice in hope of the glory of God.

*W*ithin the recesses of this verse is the key to getting off the rollercoaster of Christian living. It holds the power that we need to stand firm, never wavering with our roots dug deep, unshakeable no matter what the hurricane that surrounds us. How could I possibly say that these two little verses can hold such power over sin? Let me help you to understand by carefully dissecting this out for you. Oh, that God give me the wisdom and the words to make this truth real to you so that it may transform your life forever.

"Therefore being justified by faith" begins these two verses. Wherever there is a therefore, we need to look to what has been said before since the basis of this statement comes as a direct inevitable conclusion to what has already been said. Paul in the chapters 1 through 4 has laid out in great detail man's dilemma as a sinner with no means of earning merit by his own works. He demonstrates God's absolute justice and wrath against sin. Carefully, He lays out God's plan of redemption by Jesus Christ receiving on Himself God's full fury for our sins; thus, paying our penalty once and forever by His death on the cross with separation from God the Father for a time. He then rises from the dead, victorious against Satan and all his armies to be lifted up next to the Father full of GLORY and HONOR and Dominion. He provided a way that unrighteous man might gain His righteousness and share in His Glory through faith in Him. Because of all this work being performed by the Creator of the entire Universe we may be justified by faith. Imagine He who spoke all the Galaxies into being came to earth, suffered and died that we tiny flecks of dust, so unworthy and ungrateful, might share in His full Glory one day. This is so big that it is difficult for us to even wrap our minds around such truth-it is too big for us. Yet, because of this we are declared just and righteous before Him, not because of anything we have done, but because of everything He has done. Our only act, is to see His Glory, to believe that He is and by faith accept this wondrous gift that He has given. There is no room for self-pride in our adoption as His child, only awe that He would choose me with all my flaws. "Therefore, because of all of this redemptive work completed by God we are justified (declared innocent or guiltless; absolved; acquitted) by faith in the one who paid our price for sin to the only true Just and Righteous Judge-God.

By faith in Jesus Christ and through His power and might, we "have peace with God." His entire just wrath against sin has been satisfied by the atonement of His son, so that we might enjoy peaceful, joyful communion with God. Instead of the wrath we would deserve, we now have His full blessing. Jeremiah 29: "¹¹For I know the thoughts that I think toward you, saith the LORD, thoughts of peace, and not of evil, to give you an expected end. ¹²Then shall ye call upon me, and ye shall go and pray unto me, and I will hearken unto you" By the justification of Jesus Christ, we are moved into the position of being sons and joint heirs with Christ of everything He has. Romans Chapter 8 tells us "¹⁴For as many as are led by the Spirit of God, they are the sons of God. [15]For ye have not received the spirit of bondage again to fear; but ye have received the Spirit of adoption, whereby we cry, Abba, Father. [16]The Spirit itself beareth witness with our spirit, that we are the children of God: [17]And if children, then heirs; heirs of God, and joint-heirs with Christ; if so be that we suffer with him, that we may be also glorified together." As part of this package of peace we have been provided with the Holy Spirit who reminds us of this promise of peace. Christ promised this peace in John 14: "[26]But the Comforter, which is the Holy Ghost, whom the Father will send in my name, he shall teach you all things, and bring all things to your remembrance, whatsoever I have said unto you. [27]Peace I leave with you, my peace I give unto you: not as the world giveth, give I unto you. Let not your heart be troubled, neither let it be afraid. [28]Ye have heard how I said unto you, I go away, and come again unto you. If ye loved me, ye would rejoice, because I said, I go unto the Father: for my Father is greater than I

Through Jesus Christ "we have access by faith into this grace wherein we stand." Please listen very closely to this. By faith in Jesus Christ we have access into grace which is the force that makes us stand firmly in our Christian walk and reconfirms and circles back to fill our faith which opens our eyes more fully to Grace that holds us firm in the palm of His hand. Mercy does not give us what we deserve (death, wrath and penalty). Grace gives us what we do not deserve which is God's unmerited favor toward us. Grace which holds us up is based on the power and might of God; not by my power at all. Over and over God tells us that whosoever comes to Christ will be transformed into the image of Christ. This is found both in Romans 8: 28-29 and II Corinthians 3: 17-18. He confirms this as His work through the Holy Spirit. Having been saved by Jesus Christ and His power, it does not then change that I keep myself through works of my own. Do not get me wrong here. I am not saying then to run after sin so that God's grace might be magnified. There are two major problems with that idea. First, if you are never longing after Him then I would wonder whether you had ever seen Him through the eyes of saving faith. Second, since He has confirmed that He will complete the work; He will use however much fire and chipping needed to mold you into Christ's image. I certainly do not want to be the child molded into obedience, kicking and screaming all the way. There is another important point to it being Grace that sustains us. If you indeed are seeking after Christ, then stop worrying so much about yourself and your failed attempts to follow. Again, He will complete the work and we are held by His strength, not our own. We need to rest and relax in that promise. He made a new covenant which He **will not break** to each and every person who accepts Christ as their Savior.

This covenant is recorded in Hebrews 10[10]By the which will we are sanctified through the offering of the body of Jesus Christ once for all. [11]And every priest standeth daily ministering and offering oftentimes the same sacrifices, which can never take away sins: [12]But this man, after he had offered one sacrifice for sins for ever, sat down on the right hand of God; [13]From henceforth expecting till his enemies be made his footstool. [14]For by one offering he hath <u>perfected for ever</u> them that are sanctified. [15]Whereof the Holy Ghost also is a witness to us: for after that he had said before, [16]This is the covenant that I will make with them after those days, saith the Lord, I will put my laws into their hearts, and in their minds will I write them; 17And their sins and iniquities will I remember no more. [18]Now where remission of these is, there is no more offering for sin. [19]Having therefore, brethren, boldness to enter into the holiest by the blood of Jesus, [20]By a new and living way, which he hath consecrated for us, through the veil, that is to say, his flesh; [21]And having an high priest over the house of God; [22]Let us draw near with a true heart in full assurance of faith, having our hearts sprinkled from an evil conscience, and our bodies washed with pure water. [23]Let us hold fast the profession of our <u>faith without wavering; (for he is faithful that promised;)</u>" WOW!! Christ paid the price once and for all so that we may enter in boldly to the throne of God. He commands us to hold fast the profession of our faith not because we are faithful but God is faithful who has made this promise to us. Our righteousness is held tight by the power of God who cannot and will not deny himself. So what about those moments that your faith may waiver? He still holds us. 2 Timothy 2: [13]"If we believe not, yet he abideth faithful: he cannot deny himself." Guilt and shame which continues with us after we have turned it over to God is our way of saying that Christ is not enough. Can we raise ourselves to such levels as to say I am too holy to forgive myself when God has forgiven us? Read Romans 8: "[31]What shall we then say to these things? If God be for us, who can be against us? [32]He that spared not his own Son, but delivered him up for us all, how shall he not with him also freely give us all things? [33]Who shall lay any thing to the charge of God's elect? It is God that justifieth. [34]Who is he that condemneth? It is Christ that died, yea rather, that is risen again, who is even at the right hand of God, who also maketh intercession for us." I do not have the right to condemn even myself once I have laid my sin at the feet of Christ. I am to confess my sin, then get up with my focus ever more fixed on my Gracious Savior and march forward with Him, "the author and the finisher of my faith" as quoted from Hebrews 12: [1]Wherefore seeing we also are compassed about with so great a cloud of witnesses, let us lay aside every weight, and the sin which doth so easily beset us, and let us run with patience the race that is set before us, [2]<u>Looking unto Jesus the author and finisher of our faith;</u> who for the joy that was set before him endured the cross, despising the shame, and is set down at the right hand of the throne of God. [3]For consider him that endured such contradiction of sinners against himself, lest ye be wearied and faint in your minds. [4]Ye have not yet resisted unto blood, striving against sin."

Our ability to Stand Firm is based wholly upon Grace. By that I do not wish you to imagine something soft and fragile; but rather this comes with the Mighty Power of A God who spoke the Galaxies into being with one breath. Grace reigns through Jesus with Power, Authority and Dominion over the entire Universe. That is the power that makes you stand and keeps you standing, and stand you will even in your weakest moments because God Himself is holding you there.

Romans 14: "⁴Who art thou that judgest another man's servant? to his own master he standeth or falleth. Yea, **he shall be holden up: for God is able to make him stand**."

Because of all of this, "rejoice in hope of the glory of God." Would there be any reason left not to be joyous. He saved me, He sealed me and He will finish the work of transforming me into the image of Christ. I must rejoice in the hope that I will look like Christ. Maybe not today, but I will one day look like Him in all His Glory. That hope should be enough to keep me rejoicing through whatever trial or tribulation may come my way; knowing that God is working out my perfecting and He only has my best interest at heart. Our faith which is anchored in Jesus Christ is not only for what He has already done but that this Sovereign, Omnipotent, Omniscient Savior is steady about the work of imparting His Glory to me. I see glimpses of that Glory, little changes and transformations that are forever presenting themselves in me. I, like Paul, have not yet obtained it; yet, I look more like Him today than I did 10 years ago or 20 years ago. He will complete the work He started in me by His power and might, Hallelujah, Amen. Our Faith is anchored in Jesus Christ, the same yesterday, today and tomorrow. His promises remain steady and sure; therefore, our faith is not grounded and supported by yesterday only; but sustained through today and creates steady hoping for tomorrow, joyfully awaiting the grace that will come in the future. Knowing this stabilizes us and removes that rollercoaster from our Christian Walk.

The Grace in Which I Stand

Oh feeble heart, Oh fragile soul
Where is the hope on which you hold
With all the failures of your past
Where is the faith to make you bold
Where is the faith to make you bold

There was a King though blameless He
That came to pay my penalty
And in that act He set me free
To follow Him in liberty
To follow Him in liberty

It is His love that drew me out
And in His Grace I shall not doubt
That He who started this work in me
Will finish it with a Glorious Shout
Will finish it with a Glorious Shout

One day the finished work be done
That I might look then like God's son
Sifted, shined just like pure Gold
As Glory shines forth, Glorious One
As Glory shines forth, Glorious One

And in this hope my faith conformed
I know my life will be transformed
I stand upon this future grace
So for His work my passion warmed
So for His work my passion warmed

So in this faith I firmly stand
That formed in me as God had planned
No force on earth can shake me free
My future held by God's great hand
My future held by God's great hand.